Gral der verlorenen Träume

The Grail of lost Dreams

جام رویاهای گمشده

In dieser Anthologie begegnen sich 32 Autorinnen und Autoren aus 14 Ländern, die trotz unterschiedlicher Kulturen und Herkünfte durch ihre gemeinsame Sprache, der Lyrik, verbunden sind. Alle Gedichte sind von Deutsch oder Englisch auf Persisch übersetzt. Diese interkulturelle Kommunikation hat das Ziel, Grenzen zu überwinden und ein menschenwürdiges Leben einzufordern.

In this anthology, thirty-two authors from fourteen countries have met and joined together despite their different cultures and origins through their common lingua franca, poetry. All poems are translated either from English or German into Persian. This intercultural communication aims to overcome boundaries and to demand a dignified life.

در این گلچین شعر که شامل ترجمه اشعار آلمانی و انگلیسی به زبان فارسی است، 32 شاعر از 14 کشور جهان با وجود زبان و فرهنگ متفاوت دیدگاه خود را با زبانی مشترک، یعنی شعر بیان میکنند. آرمان این گفتمان، چیرگی بر مرزهای ساختگی و آرزوی داشتن یک زندگی شایسته با کرامت انسانی است.

Impressum

1. Auflage, 2024

Verlag Akademie-der-Abenteuer
Boris Pfeiffer, Pfalzburger Straße 10, 10719 Berlin
www.verlag-akademie-der-abenteuer.de
© 2024 by Verlag Akademie-der-Abenteuer
Alle Rechte vorbehalten.
Die Rechte zur weiteren Veröffentlichung der Gedichte
über diesen Band hinaus verbleiben bei den Verfasserinnen
und Verfassern.
Nachdruck, auch auszugsweise, nicht gestattet.
Covergestaltung: Laleh Ziai
Satz: Maryam Andaz
Gedruckt und gebunden von BoD GmbH, Norderstedt
ISBN 978-3-98530-136-2
Printed in Germany

Bibliografische Information der Deutschen Nationalbibliothek:
Die Deutsche Nationalbibliothek verzeichnet diese Publikation in der
Deutschen Nationalbibliographie; detaillierte bibliografische Daten sind
Im Internet über http://dnb.d-nb.de abrufbar.

Gral der verlorenen Träume
The Grail of lost Dreams

جام رویاهای گمشده

Herausgegeben von
Nahid Ensafpour

Geleitwort

In jeder Zeile dieser Anthologie der Poesie mit dem wunderbaren Titel „Gral der verlorenen Träume" zeigt sich das Erleben eines Momentes, indem gleichzeitig die besondere Stimmung des vergänglichen Augenblicks mitschwingt. Ein „panta rhei" – alles fließt – wie Heraklit es so trefflich bezeichnete, indem sich alles fortwährend verändert und doch jeder Moment als Summe aller vorherigen Empfindungen und Erinnerungen hervorgeht und neue Momente entstehen lässt. Dadurch gelingt das Wunder, das die Poesie vermag: alles zu einem Ganzen zusammenzufügen.

Poesie ist immer eng mit einem Zeitbewusstsein verbunden. Wenn wir zurück in das 18. Jahrhundert gehen, von Gottscheds Worten, seiner Zeit und ihrem Bewusstsein ausgehen, verstehen wir, dass die Wesensbestimmung der Poesies als „Nachahmung der Natur" bezeichnet werden kann. Das Dasein selbst ist voll und ganz Poesie. Sie ist die ursprüngliche Sprache der Menschheit, ist die einzige zur Verständigung der Völker und Kulturen, ist ästhetische Kunst, die die Grenzen überwinden kann.

Melancholie in unsicheren Zeiten und die Kunst der Poesie stehen in engem Zusammenhang mit Gefühlen, oder auch dem Bewusstsein von Verlust und Vergänglichkeit. Gleichzeitig bergen sie im Nacherleben auch die Chance auf einen Neubeginn in sich.
Als verbindend zwischen Poesie und dem Bewusstwerden der Melancholie kann man auf die heutige Zeit bezogen, die Aussagen der niederländischen Philosophin Joke H. Hermsen begreifen. Sie beschreibt die Kunst und somit auch die Poesie als einen Hoffnungsträger, um Ängste und Zweifel zu überwinden

und eine neue Beziehung zu sich selbst und der Welt aufzubauen.

Dichtkunst und Melancholie bilden seit Jahrhunderten eine Einheit. Literatur, Theater, Tanz und Musik bergen in sich das Potential der Kreativität. Durch die Kunst der Poesie ist es möglich, etwas von unserem Selbst zu erkennen. Diesem Selbst, welches die Sehnsucht nach einer unerreichbaren Vergangenheit genauso in sich birgt, wie ein Verlangen, einen Traum, der trotz allen Wissens um seine Nichterfüllung in uns bestehen bleibt. Es ist die Poesie, durch die es gelingt, grenzenlos zu werden. Sie schafft es eine Verbundenheit zwischen den Menschen und gleichzeitig eine sich ständig verändernde Beziehung zu einem bewussteren, sich erneuernden „Ich" aufzunehmen.

Nahid Ensafpour habe ich bei Ihrem wunderbaren Vortrag „Poetik und Melancholie" in meinem Seminar „Ich weiß nicht, was soll es bedeuten … über die Melancholie in unsicheren Zeiten" lauschen dürfen. Ich danke Dir, liebe Nahid, für das mir entgegengebrachte Vertrauen, diese Anthologie begleiten zu dürfen und wünsche allen Kreativen weiterhin, aus Ihren Ideen Kraft und Mut zu fassen und dies auch durch ihre Worte vermitteln zu können.

Frankfurt am Main im Februar 2023
Dr. phil. Elke Wehrs
https:www.elkewehrs.de

Preface

Each line of this presented anthology of poetry with the beautiful title „Grail of Lost Dreams" shows the experience of a moment in which simultaneously the specific mood of the fleeting moment resonates. A „panta rhei" – everything flows – as Heraclitus so aptly called it, in which everything is constantly changing, and each moment emerges as the sum of all previous sensations and memories and gives rise to new moments. All this achieves the miracle that poetry can do: to put everything together into a whole.

Poetry is always closely linked to a consciousness of time. If we go back to the 18th century, starting from Gottsched's words, his time, and his consciousness, we will understand that the essence of poetry as an „imitation of nature" can be designed. Dasein itself is poetry in its entirety. It is the original language of humanity, is the only one for understanding people and cultures, and is aesthetic art that can transcend boundaries.

Melancholy in uncertain times and the art of poetry are closely related to senses, or the awareness of loss and transience. At the same time, they also hold the chance for a new beginning in the afterlife.

The statements of the Dutch philosopher Joke H. Hermsen show that the problems of our present times are better perceived in the context of a connection between poetry and the awareness of melancholy. She describes art, and thus poetry too, as a beacon of hope to overcome fears and doubt and build a new relationship with oneself and the world.

Poetry and melancholy have formed a unity for centuries. Literature, theatre, dance, and music hold the potential for creativity. Through poetry, it is possible to recognize something of ourselves. This self contains the longing for an unattainable past and a desire, a dream that remains in us despite all the knowledge of its non-fulfilment. It is poetry through which it is possible to become limitless. It creates a bond between the people and a constantly changing relationship with a more conscious, renewed „I" simultaneously.

I had a chance to listen to Nahid Ensafpour's outstanding lecture on „Poetics and Melancholy" in my seminar on "I do not know what it means … about the melancholy in insecure times". Thank you so much, dear Nahid, for the trust shown in me to be allowed to accompany this anthology, and I wish all creative authors to continue to draw on their ideas to gain strength and courage and to be able to convey this to everyone through their words.

Frankfurt am Main, February 2023
Ph. D. Elke Wehrs
Translated into English: Jana Machacova

پیشگفتار

هر سطر این مجموعه شعر با عنوان زیبای «جام رویاهای گمشده» گویای لحظه هایی گذرا از زندگی-ست. همانگونه که هراکلیت به درستی بیان می کند، "Santa hei" یعنی همه چیز در جریان و در حال تغییر است. در این رابطه می توان گفت که هر لحظه از زندگی نشانگر همه احساسات و دربرگیرنده خاطرات گذشته است که دوران جدید از درون آن پدید می آید

یکی از شگفتی های ویژه شعر نیز این است که شامل همه این لحظات می باشد. شعر همواره پیوند تنگاتنگی با هر دوره زندگی دارد. اگر به قرن هجدهم برگردیم و سخنان گاتشدز Gottscheds را که نشانگر ویژگی آن دوره است مورد بررسی قراردهیم، می فهمیم شعر تعریف او از شعر چیست. به گفته او شعر را می توان «تقلید از طبیعت» توصیف کرد

زندگی و هستی خود نشانه ای از شعر است و به زبان دیگر شعر خود زندگی ست. شعر عنصر زبان اولیه بشری ست، زبانی ست برای تفاهم بین انسان ها و فرهنگ آنها، هنری ست زیبایی شناسانه که قادر به برداشتن همه مرزهاست مِلانکولی[1] و شعر در شرایط ناپایدار و درحال گذار زندگی، ارتباط تنگاتنگی با احساسات و دانش بشر دارد و همواره در حالیکه وقایع گذشته را دربرمی گیرد شانسی است برای آغازی نوین

همانگونه که فیلسوف هلندی جوک اچ. هرمزن Jock H. Hermsen در رابطه با شناخت مِلانکولی در شرایط امروزی بیان می کند، مشکلات حقیقی زندگی روزمره ما در قالب شعر بهتر قابل درک است. به گفته او هنر و شعر نور امیدی برای غلبه بر ترس و ایجاد ارتباطی جدید با خود و جهان می باشد.

شعر و مِلانکولی از دیرزمان با یکدیگر پیوندی ناگسستنی دارند. همچنین در ادبیات و همه هنرها از جمله تئاتر، رقص، موسیقی و غیره چنین پیوندی نیز وجود دارد که دارای پتانسیل بُروز خلاقیت اند. با هنر شعر می توان به خودشناسی رسید. خودی که آرزوی رسیدن به گذشته دست نیافتنی را در خویش پنهان دارد، مانند آرزویی که با آگاهی به برآورده نشدنش همچنان در ما برجای می ماند. یکی از ویژگی های شعر شکستن مرزها در ضمیر انسانی ست. شعر

قـادر بـه ایجـاد ارتبـاط بیـن انسـان-هاسـت. ایـن ارتبـاط همیشـه در حـال تغییـر و تکامـل و همـراه بـا شـناخت نویـن از جهـان پیرامـون اسـت

در پایـان مایلـم از دوسـت عزیـزم ناهیـد انصـاف پـور - کـه از سـخنرانی او در دانشـگاه فرانکفـورت در سـمینار شـعر و ملانکولـی بسـیار اسـتفاده کـردم بخاطـر دعـوت از مـن بـرای نـوشتن مقدمـه ایـن کتـاب سپاسـگزاری کنـم همچنیـن بـرای همـه هنرمنـدان خلاق ایـن مجموعـه شـعر آرزو مـی کنـم کـه بتواننـد در آینـده نیـز ایـده هـای خـود را بـی باکانـه در قالـب واژه هـا بیـان کننـد.

دکتر الکه ورز Dr. Phil. Elke Wehrs
فرانکفورت، فوریه 2023

۱- واژه ملانکولی Melancholie در اینجا ترجمه نشده، زیرا ترجمه این واژه در لغت نامه های فارسی به معنی "مالیخولیایی" است. تعریف واژه مالیخولیا یعنی فردی که دچار Depressو مشکلات روحی است. کاربرد واژه ملانکولی به زبان آلمانی در سال های اخیر عوض شده و معنی آن فقط انسانی اندوهگین است که مشکل روحی و روانی ندارد. این واژه در هنر و ادبیات معنای دقیق تری دارد. انسانی که دچار ملانکولی است می تواند در بهترین شرایط اندوه و درد خود را به خلاقیت هنری تبدیل کند و دست به آفرینش هنری بزند. بطور مثال می شود از گفته ارسطو در این مورد یاد کرد: ملانکولی منشاء و سرچشمه آفرینش هنری انسان است.

Vorwort

"Übersetzer sind als geschäftige Kuppler anzusehen, die uns eine halbverschleierte Schöne als höchstliebenswürdig anpreisen: sie erwecken eine unwiderstehliche Neigung nach dem Original." [2]

J.W. von Goethe

Die Idee, eine Anthologie aus den Gedichten meiner internationalen Freunde, übersetzt in Farsi, zu publizieren, war ein Wagnis. Es ist bekannt, dass die Übersetzung eines literarischen Textes beachtliche Voraussetzungen erfordert. Um eine möglichst textnahe Übersetzung zu erschaffen, ist es unerlässlich, die Sprache, die Kultur der jeweiligen Länder, aus denen die Gedichte stammen, wie auch die Autorinnen und Autoren selbst gut zu kennen.

Die Originaltexte erhielt ich in Deutsch. Bei der Hälfte der Gedichte allerdings handelte es sich dabei nicht um die Originalversionen, sondern um bereits zuvor auf Englisch übersetzte Texte. Dies war natürlich ein Hindernis, die Gedankenwelt der Autoren direkt zu erfahren. Doch ich hoffe, dies gemeistert zu haben.

Um eine andere Schwierigkeit bei der Kunst der Übersetzung deutlich zu machen, möchte ich die Ansichten von zwei bekannten deutschen Literaturhistorikern und Philosophen zu Rate ziehen.

August Wilhelm Schlegel (1767-1845) hebt bezüglich der poetischen Übersetzung hervor, dass die „eigentliche Übersetzung" keine „Nachschöpfung", sondern eine „Neuschöpfung" ist, welche als „Poesie der Poesie" bezeichnet werden kann.

Walter Benjamin (1892-1940) betont in diesem Kontext, dass nicht der Inhalt eines Gedichtes dieses zu einem wertvollen Kunstwerk macht, sondern dass das Wesentliche „das Unfassbare, Geheimnisvolle, Dichterische"[3] ist.

Allen Fragen und Zweifeln zum Trotz - die Übersetzung dieser Gedichte von 32 Autorinnen und Autoren aus 14 Ländern empfand ich als eine einzigartige Reise durch Gedankenwelten, deren poetische Gestaltungsmittel nicht verschiedener hätten sein könnte. Und dies wiederum ermutigte mich, mir meine eigene Sprache im Übersetzungsprozess neu anzueignen und bisweilen die Werke wahrhaftig nachzudichten.

Ich habe mich insgesamt immer bemüht, soweit es mir möglich war, den Inhalt und den klanglichen Charakter der Gedichte getreu wiederzugeben. Ich möchte mich an dieser Stelle herzlich bei allen Lyrikerinnen und Lyrikern bedanken, die mir ihre wunderbaren Gedichte anvertrauten. Durch die Übersetzung eurer Werke habe ich neue Entdeckungen und Erkenntnisse gewinnen können.

Dann möchte ich mich bei meiner geliebten Schwester Nasrin Ensafpour von ganzem Herzen bedanken, da sie die von mir übersetzten Texte in Farsi lektoriert hat. Meine liebe Freundin Jana Machacova hat die Übersetzungen des Vorworts und des Geleitworts von Dr. Elke Wehrs auf Englisch übernommen. Ihr gilt ebenso mein besonderer Dank. Und selbstverständlich geht mein Dank auch an meine liebe Freundin Dr. Elke Wehrs, die diese Anthologie mit ihrem Gleitwort geschmückt hat. Mein besonderer Dank gilt ebenfalls der Künstlerin Laleh Ziai, die als Karikaturistin, Designerin, Cartoonistin und Illustratorin arbeitet, für Ihre Gestaltung des Umschlags.

Nahid Ensafpour/ August 2023

---

[2] Jans Joachim Störig [Hrsg.]: Das Problem des Übersetzens, S. 7.
[3] Walter Benjamin: Gesammelte Schriften IV. Hrsg. Tillman Rexroth. Frankfurt am Main: Suhrkamp Verlag 1972, S.9.

Foreword

„Translators are like busy matchmakers who praise us a half-veiled beauty as most amiable; they arouse an irresistible inclination towards the original." [4]

J.W. von Goethe

The idea of publishing an anthology of poems written by my international friends, translated by me into Farsi, was an act of real courage. It is well-known that the translation of a text, especially if it is a poem, entails considerable prerequisites.

It is essential to have good language skills, knowledge of the culture of the respective countries, and to know the authors themselves well to a certain extent to achieve a good translation that is as close to the original text as possible.

I received the original texts in German. About half of the poems were not in their original, but texts translated into English. This fact was itself an obstacle to learning directly from the world of thought of the authors.

To clearly show the difficulty of poetic translation, I would like to refer to the views of two well-known German literary historians and philosophers.

For example, about poetic translation, Schlegel points out that the „actual translation" is not a „re-creation" but a „new creation", which can be as the „poetry of poetry" described.

Furthermore, Walter Benjamin emphasizes in this context that the content of a poem does not make a poem a valuable work of art, but "the incomprehensible, mysterious, "poetic" „ is essential.[5]

Despite all the questions and doubts, I found the translation of the poems of thirty-two authors from fourteen countries like a unique journey through the world of thoughts of these authors, whose poetic means of expression in poetry could not have been more different. However, I hope to have mastered this successfully.

I have dared to embark on this journey and have endeavoured, as far as possible, to faithfully reproduce the content and the tonal character of chosen poems.

At this point, I would like to thank all the poets who entrusted me with their beautiful poems. Through the process of translation of your poems, I was able to find some discoveries and new insights.

I should like to express my heartfelt gratitude to my beloved sister Nasrin Ensafpour for editing the texts I translated into Farsi. Next, I would also like to thank my dear friend Jana Machacova for translations of my foreword and the introduction by Dr Elke Wehrs from German into English.

Finally, I also wish to thank my dear friend Dr Elke Wehrs, who adorned our anthology with her magnificent preface. My special thanks also go to the artist Laleh Ziai (caricaturist, designer, cartoonist, and illustrator) for designing the cover of our anthology.

Nahid Ensafpour/ August 2023
Translated into English: Jana Machakova

---

[4] Jans Joachim Storing (Hrsg.): Das Problem des Übersetzens, S.7.
[5] Walter Benjamin: Gesammelte Schriften IV. Hg. Tillmann Rexroth. Frankfurt am Main: Suhrkamp Verlag 1972, S.9.

دیباچه

یوهان ولفگانگ گوته .J.W. Goethe معتقد است که: «مترجمان را می توان مانند حلقه واسطی دید که قادرند تنها نیمی از راز زیبایی پشتِ پرده را ببینند و ستایش کنند. برای آنان شوق به درک مطلبی به زبانی دیگر، انگیزه ای قوی در ترجمه است.»

ایده انتشار این مجموعه شعر از دوستان شاعرم درعرصه بین المللی تصمیم دشواری بود. چرا که ترجمه یک متن خارجی بخصوص اگر آن متن یک شعر باشد، مستلزم شناخت زبان و فرهنگ کشور شاعر و همچنین شناخت خود شاعرمی باشد تا بتوان آن شعر را تا حد ممکن نزدیک به اصل ترجمه کرد

نیمی از شعرهای دریافت شده از شاعران در این کتاب به زبان آلمانی و از شاعران آلمانی زبان است که ترجمه آنها از روی اصل متن بوده، ولی نیم دیگر شعرهای دریافت شده از شاعران دیگر به زبان انگلیسی ست که از زبانی دیگر به انگلیسی ترجمه شده اند و این خود مانند سدی بین مترجم دوم و شاعر است که درنتیجه کار ترجمه را تا حدی دشوارتر کرده است

برای درک دشواری ترجمه شعر و امکان یک ترجمه خوب در اینجا به دیدگاه دو ادیب و فیلسوف مشهور آلمانی اشاره می شود: اگوست ویلهلم شلگل August Wilhelm Schlegel، دراین مورد معتقد است که ترجمه واقعی یک شعر بازآفرینی نیست، بلکه خود یک آفرینش نو است. به زبان دیگر می توان گفت مانند سُرودن شعر از روی شعری دیگر است.

والتربنیامین Walter Benjamin، نیزدراین زمینه تاکید می کند که ترجمه محتوای یک شعر، شعر را به یک اثر هنری با ارزش تبدیل نمی کند، بلکه آنچه مهم است راز درونی غیرقابل بیان در شعر، در ورای درک صوری آن است. به زبان دیگر همان اسانس شاعرانه آن

ترجمه اشعار 32 شاعر از 14 کشور جهان با سروده های کاملا متفاوت، برایم سفری بسیار شگفت انگیز به دنیای اندیشه این نویسندگان بود که مرا واداشت تا در شیوه ترجمه، زبان خود را با روش جدیدی تطبیق دهم، تا آنگاه اگر افکار شاعری برایم کاملا روشن نبود، آن شعر را بازآفرینی کنم.

برای پای گذاشتن به این سفر با همه دشواری هایش سعی شد تا آنجا که ممکن است محتوا و ساختار شعرها و آهنگ خوانش شان نزدیک به اصل مطلب، بازآفرینی شود.

در اینجا مایلم از همه شاعرانی که اشعارشان را برای ترجمه در اختیارم گذاشتند صمیمانه تشکر کنم. ترجمه این اشعار مرا به سفری شگفت انگیز برد که دستاورد آن شناخت و دستیابی به دیدگاه های نوینی بود

در پایان سپاس بیکران دارم از خواهر عزیزم نسرین انصاف پور برای ویرایش ترجمه این اشعار به زبان فارسی و همچنین سپاس فراوان از دوست گرامی ام یانا ماخاکووا Jana Machacova برای ترجمه پیشگفتار دکتر الکه ورز Dr. Elke Wehrs از زبان آلمانی به انگلیسی و نیز ترجمه دیباچه مترجم. با سپاس بیکران از دوست گرامی ام دکتر الکه ورز Dr. Elke Wehrs برای آراستن این کتاب با پیشگفتار فوق العاده شان و نیز مایلم از لاله ضیایی کاریکاتوریست، طراح و تصویرگر توانا برای طراحی جلد این کتاب تشکر کنم

ناهید انصاف پور / اگوست 2023

فهرست نویسندگان

Author index

Autorenindex

Mária Bátorová (Slovakia), Soledad Benages (Spain), Giovanna Benedetti (Panama/ Spain), Dieter Brumm (Germany), Antonio Capilla Loma (Spain), Metin Cengiz (Turkey), Nahid Ensafpour (Iran/ Germany), Silvia Cuevas-Morales (Chile/ Spain), Maria do Sameiro Barroso (Portugal), Hasan Erkek (Turkey), Gertrud Hauck (Austria), Heidi Heine (Germany), Petra Jansen (Germany), Bahar Kazemi (Germany/ Iran), Jutta Lehmann (Germany), Helene Levar (Austria), Marta Markoska (Macedonia), Erwin Matl (Austria), Sylvia Meise (Germany), Maria Lucilia Meleiro (Portugal), Isabel Miguel (Spain), Ana Montojo (Spain), Julio Pavanetti, (Uruguay/ Spain), Ljubica Perkman (Bosnia/ Germany), Boris Pfeiffer (Germany), Kheder Salfij (Syria), Agron Shele (Albania/ Belgium), Andy Siege (Germany/ Iran), Nasrin Siege (Iran/ Germany), Antje Stehn, (Germany/ Italy), Annabel Villar (Uruguay/ Spain), Peter Voelker (Germany).

فهرست — Inhaltsverzeichnis

کِرتا	28	Kreta
در خفا	30	Heimlich
بر گور فرزند	34	Das Grab eines Kindes
شب	36	Nacht
نسیم پایان تابستان	40	Septemberwind
رویاها	42	Träume
شناور	46	Treibgut
جزیره ای زیر باران	48	Insel im Regen
بُهتان	52	Rufmord
اینجا و آنجا	58	Hier und Da
آرزو	60	Sehnsucht
نپرسید چرا	64	Fragt nicht warum
اگر خاموشی پیشه کنم	66	Wenn ich die Stille zulasse
نیایشی با فرشته نجات	70	Gebet zum Schutzengel
دگرگونی	74	Veränderung
آفتاب	76	Sonnenstrahlen
برپا خیز	80	Aufstehen
گوش سپردن به تو	84	Dir zuzuhören ist…
در امتداد شب	86	Ich male dir Herzschläge
میخواهم بپوشانم پیکرت رابا برگ های پاییزی	88	Ich möchte dich mit Herbstlaub bedecken
وطن آواره	92	Heimatlos
بوسه یک دم	94	Kuss des Augenblicks
بودن در این مکان	96	Da sein ist nicht hier sein
روز یادبود هولوکاست	100	Gedenktag Holocaust
در این آشفته بازار	102	Wo Sinnfetzenfinden
سالهای از دست رفته	106	Verflossene Jahreszeiten
نشان رستگاری	108	Spuren der Erlösung
غروب	113	Dämmerung
در امتداد کوچه شوربختی	116	In die Straßen der Elenden hinaus
شعر چون سلاح	121	Poetry, that weapon
در ژرفای تنهایی	125	Epicentre of the loneliness

131	Pavilion of the rose	گلستانی از گل رُز
135	Everything from nothing	هستی از درون نیستی
141	I drank the grail of lost dreams	جام رویاهای گمشده
145	The wall	دیوار
151	Rose	گل رُز
154	What time has us say	پیامِ زمان
159	Going back home	بازگشت به وطن
164	September 11 th, 1973	سپتامبر1973-11
171	A bird across my face	پرنده ای در برابر دیدگانم
174	Add me to your poem	مرا به شعرت اضافه کن
179	Painted birds	پرنده های رنگ شده
183	The bleeding wings of love	بال خونین عشق
189	End of the World	پایان دنیا
192	Quantum theory of love	تئوری کوانتُم عشق
197	To unleash the words	برای رهایی کلمات
200	The endless knots	گره های بی پایان
205	Where the tear	کجاست اشکی
208	I do not feel guilty	احساس گناه نمی کنم
213	Water	آب
216	Winter	زمستان
221	In a Verse	در یک شعر
225	Nightly	شب ها
231	Ich wünschte mir	ای کاش
234	Es ist niemals zu spät	هرگز دیر نیست
239	Armies	سربازان
242	Lake death	مرگ دریا
247	Passage	گذرگاه
250	How far away and nearby	چه غریب، چه آشنا
254	Mirror	آینه
256	Lunatic Moon	ماه سرگشته
261	In transit	آستانه
264	Alice behind the mirror	آلیس در پشت آینه

Dieter J. G. Brumm
Germany

Kreta

Tanzende Olivenstämme,
Platanen über den Schluchten
der Lefka Ori –
Steinschleudern
aus dem Eozän –:
vor all dem Hominidenwahn.

In zerfallenen Palästen
hörst du
vielleicht noch ihre Stimmen;
doch seit Zeus nach Europa griff,
bleiben
auch Hieroglyphen stumm.

Und die Angst?
In Stein gehauen,
wurde sie zum Denkmal
toter Wälder.
Allein
Wildblütengesänge
zum Küstenwind,
oder schwellende Bougainvilleen,
heben Vergangenheit auf.

Denn geschundene Orte,
das immer wieder
gemordete Paradies
im Meer:
Die Götter haben es
noch nicht verlassen.

کِرِتا[6]

رقص درختان زیتون
درختان چنار
بر فراز دره های لفکااوری[7]
تیر و کمان کودکانه ائوسن[8]
پیش از جنون هومینیدها[9]
در ویرانه های باستانی شان
می توان شنید
شاید هنوز صدای شان را

اما آن زمان
که زئوس[10] به اروپا آمد
حتی خاموش می ماند
خط هیروگلیف شان

ترسی
که بر سنگ ها حک شده
یادآور مرگ جنگل هاست

تنها آهنگ رقص شکوفه های وحشی
در باد ساحل
یا گل های به شکوفه نشسته بوگنویل ها
می تواند بزداید
گناهان گذشته را

این مکان ننگین
جایگاه جنایت دوباره
همواره قبرستانی ست بهشت آسا
در دل دریا
که خدایان ترکش نکرده اند هنوز.

---

[6] کِرِتا Kreta ، یکی از بزرگترین جزایر یونان. قبرستان مهاجرانی که به اروپا سفر می کنند.
[7] لفکااوری Lefka Ori ، کوه های اطراف جزیره کرتا در یونان.
[8] ائوسن Eozean ، یکی از دوره های زمین شناسی است که از 33/9 تا 56 میلیون سال پیش گفته می شود.
[9] هومینیدها Hominiden ، پیشینیان اولین خانواده انسانی که ژن مشترک با اورنگ اوتان ها و شمپانزه ها دارند.
[10] زئوس Zeus ، خدای خدایان در اساطیر یونانی.

Heimlich

Wo die Blaulichttannen schweigen
und kein Stern den andren hält,
tanzen Totenvögel Reigen,
weil die Welt in Scherben fällt.

Grabesstille allenthalben,
nur die Angst der Städte schreit:
Ihre Seelen sind die Schwalben
dieser neuen Dunkelheit.

Aus den Mooren, von den Bergen
steigt wie Regen ihre Schuld;
keiner kann sich mehr verbergen:
heimlich stirbt der Sonnenkult.

در خفا

آنگاه که کاج های درخشانِ آبی
سکوت می کنند
و ستارگان، بی پناه و سرگردانند
گروهی از مرده پرندگان می رقصند
چرا که جهان به پرتگاه تاریکی
افتاده
سکوتِ مرگبار حاکم بر دنیا
ترس و وحشت شهرها را
که روح شان
پرستوهای این سیاهی نوظهورند
فریاد می زنند

بر کوه ها و چمن ها می بارد
گناهان شان چون باران،
دیگر مجالی نیست
برای پنهان شدن

آیین ستایش نور
می میرد اما در خفا.

Nahid Ensafpour
Iran/ Germany

Das Grab eines Kindes

(für die unbekannte Mutter)

In der Stille des Friedhofs
wo im Schweigen
tausende Worte
verborgen sind
und jede Regung
sie erschüttert
saß eine Frau
am Grabe ihres Kindes
versunken in sich
sah Bilder
Erinnerungen

Mit tiefem Schmerz
und trüben Augen
blickte sie ins Nichts
und dachte
dass alles auf Erden
dem Nichts gleicht

Vor ihren verwunderten
Augen
flatterte tanzend
ein Schmetterling
über ihre Hand

برای مادری گمنام

بر گور فرزند

در خاموشی وهمناک گورستان
در سکوتی
با بسیار سخن های ناگفته
بر لب
که خش خش برگی همهمه ای ست
نشسته مادری بر گورِ فرزندش
غرقه در خود فرو
با مرور تصویرها و یادها

در ژرفای درد
با نگاهی سرد
خیره می نگرد
به انتهای تهی

در اندیشه اش
زندگی برگرفته از هیچ...

ناگاه در برابر چشمان بی فروغِ او
پروانه ای
پر کشیده
و می رقصد
در میان دست هایش
می چرخد،
می رقصد
می چرخد
می رقصد...

Nacht

Langsam flüchtet
der Tag hinter die Berge
es ist als käme
die Nacht
leise durch die Tür
und küsse wie eine Mutter
sanft ihr Kind
sie zieht ringsum
ihren dunklen Vorhang

Bäume neigen sich
nach vorne
Vögel werden still
und lauschen sacht
Dunkelheit legt sich
auf die ganze Natur
der Wald atmet still
und ruht
die Nacht lauert auf
den Tagesanbruch
sie verliert sich
nach und nach
bei der Umarmung
der Vergangenheit
und Zukunft

شب

روز می گریزد به آرامی
پشت کوه ها
شب چون مادری
برای بوسیدن کودکش
پاورچین باز می کند در را
و به هر سوی می کشد پرده سیاهش را

درختان فرورفته در خود
پرندگان خاموش
گوش می سپارند
به نوای آرام طبیعت

تاریکی بر جهان حاکم
جنگل در خواب سنگین
و در رویا

در کمین سپیده دم
آنگاه
ذره ذره محو می شود شب
در هم آغوشِ گذشته
و آینده.

Gertrud Hauck
Austria

Septemberwind

Sommer verschollen
Sonne abgängig
Himmel wolkenverhangen
Kein Sommerwind streichelt Körper
kalte Winde umwehen
Gefühle erstarren

Norden, Osten, Süden, Westen
Grausamkeiten ersonnen
Nicht durch eines Gottes Willen
Machthungrige programmieren
Menschliche Roboter
Hass gesteuerte Köpfe
Verzerrte Gesichter

Maschinengewehrstakkato
Bombengedröhne
Raketenschwangere Luft
Flugzeuge bersten
Körper verstümmelt verstreut
Menschenwürde geächtet
Kriege zerstören wieder Frieden

Septemberwind
Still unsere Sehnsucht

Verblase Kriege und Hass
Vermenschliche Roboter
Bring Köpfen
Vernunft und Einsicht
Gib Seelen Zufriedenheit.

نسیم پایان تابستان

پایان تابستان
خورشید، رنگ باخته
آسمان ابری و تیره
آرزوی نسیم گرم نوازشگر
وزش باد سرد
و احساسات یخ زده

زور و ستم
حاکم بر
شمال، شرق، جنوب، غرب
نه خواست خدا
که خواست حاکمان است
و انسان های ماشینی
با مغزهایی پر از نفرت
و چهره هایی مصنوعی
مسلسل های استاکو
پهپادهای بمب افکن
و آسمانی پر از موشک
هواپیماهای نابود کننده
بدن های پاره پاره شده

تحقیر کرامت انسانی
نابودی دوباره صلح.

نسیمِ گرمِ پایانِ تابستان!
برآورده کن آرزوها را
محو کن جنگ و نفرت را
انسان کن
این انسان واره ها را
با بینش و خِرَد
آرامش ده به جان ها.

Träume

Träume entstehen,
Suche nach Glück,
Beziehungen blühen,
Lichter erlöschen,
Tränen vor Gräbern,
Träume unerfüllt.

Katastrophen erschüttern,
Kriege verstören,
Entsetzen beherrscht Welt,
Tausende Leben verloschen,
Trauer vor Gräbern
Unvorstellbare Dimensionen.

Realität
Unerfüllte Träume
Banalität

Erkenntnis
Bedeutung von Glück -
Gesundheit,
Zufriedenheit,
Besitzen
Was Andere
Verloren
- Leben.

رویاها

رویایی در سر
در جستجوی خوشبختی
شکوفایی دوستی ها
و ناگهان خاموشی چراغ ها
گریه بر مزار مردگان
رویای دست نیافتنی

فجایع تکان دهنده
جنگ های مصیبت زا
وحشت حاکم بر دنیا

چه بسیار
زندگی های از دست رفته
سوگواری در کنار مزارها
با وسعتی غیرقابل تصور

چه بی رنگ شد
سودای این رویاها

خوشبختی چیست؟
سلامتی و خشنودی
از آنچه که داریم
و آنچه که دیگران
از دست داده اند
- زندگی.

Heidi Heine
Germany

Treibgut

Am Ufer meiner Träume
liege ich
-angeschwemmtes Treibgut –
dürstend nach Heimat
offener Schoß für Traumgebilde,
es zieht mich nach kleiner Insel
mitten im wogenden Ozean.

شناور

در ساحل رویاهایم
چون جسمی شناور
بر روی آب
تشنه جایی امن
خانه ای، وطنی
با آغوشی باز
برای تصویری خیالی
در جستجوی
جزیره کوچکی
در میان اقیانوسی
پرتلاطم.

Insel im Regen

Seh' nur sanfte Hügel
im gelben Grün.
Seh' Himmel und Regen
im Meer erblüh'n.

Still steht die Zeit,
atmet kaum.
Smaragden ihr Kleid,
Seide und Samt im Saum.

Sag, find ich zurück,
streif ab dies Gewand?
Vielleicht bleibt mir ein Stück
von Seide und Samt?

جزیره ای زیر باران

بنگر رنگ سبز و زردِ تپه های زیبا را
بنگر جلوه آسمان و باران
در دریا را

زمان ایستاده از حرکت
می کشد به سختی نفس
لباسش به رنگ زمرد
دوخته از مخمل و ابریشم

بگو آیا می یابم راه بازگشت را
تا برجای گذارم این جامه را؟
شاید باز ماند برایم
پاره ای از آن مخمل و ابریشم.

Petra Jansen
Germany

Rufmord

Ans Kreuz genagelt, Opfer der Boshaftigkeit.
Gespaltene Zungen wetzen die Messer,
ein Zucken durch humanitäre Gefühle.
Aussagen geben den Stich des Todes.
Unwiderruflich. Von jetzt auf gleich.
Rein in die Scheiße.
Machtlos reißt du deine Augen auf,
das Wort versackt in der trockenen Kehle.
Und nun?
Kein Richterspruch der Welt nimmt
den klebrigen Ballast
von Deinen Schultern.
Der Makel pappt ewig fest.
Gaffa ist ein Dreck dagegen. Dabei so gut gemeint.
So verdammt lieb gemeint. Einfach lieb.
Herzlich, menschlich, ganz normal. Wie es halt so ist.
Ganz und gar nicht ungewöhnlich.
Der Hass traf leider dich.
Verleumdungsklage löst nicht den Stempel.
Nie mehr wieder.
Nie! Nie! Nie!
Für den du gar nichts konntest.
Die Institution war schuld.
Hass, dessen Zielscheibe du eigentlich nicht warst.
Hat niemand drüber nachgedacht.
Hass denkt nie.
Nie! Nie! Nie!
Du setzt deinen Fuß nicht mehr in diese Tür.
Sie wurde aus den Angeln gehoben,
der Teufel ist hindurch geschritten.
Da hängst du nun am Kreuz.
Deine Taten waren: Wahrheit und ganz einfach Liebe.
Rostige Nägel bohren sich blutend durch das Fleisch.
Du leidest.

Was interessiert es den Pöbel?
Die Geschichte ist nicht tot.
Lebendiger denn je.

بُهتان

میخکوب بر صلیب
قربانی شرارت
زبان ها اهریمنی
دشنه ها تیز
تلنگری به حس بشردوستانه
سخن ها مَرگ زا.

حُکمی بازگشت ناپذیر
به ناگاه، افتاده در گنداب
بی اختیار چشمانت را باز کرده
واژه ها خشکیده در گلو

و اکنون
حُکم هیچ دادگاهی این بار سنگین را
از دوش تو برنمی دارد
این لکه ای ست که تا ابد می ماند
این مُهرِ بهتان اما، ننگین تر از آن لکه

با نیت خیر، با حس خوب
از ته قلب، انسانی، کاملا عادی،
همانگونه که معمول است
و غیرعادی نیست
نفرتی که از بختِ بد، تو را جُست

مُهر بُهتان پاک نمی شود، نه هرگز
هرگز! هرگز! هرگز!
چرا که تو بی گناهی
این گناه دستگاه قدرت بود
تنفری که تو هدف آن نبودی
کسی به آن فکر نمی کرد
تنفر تفکر را برنمی تابد

هرگز! هرگز! هرگز!

تو دیگر بر آستان این در پا نمی گذاری
دری که از جا کنده شده
و شیطان از آستان آن گذر کرده است

اکنون آویخته بر صلیب
گناه تو: حقیقت و عشق

با میخ های زنگ زده
سوراخ شده، پیکرِ رنجورِ تو
رنج تو را چه به عوام؟
تاریخ همچنان زنده است
زنده تر از همیشه.

Bahar Kazemi
Germany/ Iran

Hier und Da

Vor meinen Augen
das Hier und Dort
Transparenz als Grenze
im Strudel ihres Seins
offenbaren mir
das Hier und Dort
Seite an Seite
mein Selbst
welches sich versteckte
im Herzen meines Zwiespalts.

Transparenz,
welche empor streckt die Arme
ist es schließlich
die mein Selbst werden lässt zur Tür
zwischen dem Hier und Dort,
bereit um zu empfangen
Gewissheit,
deren Macht zerbrechen lässt
die zarte Hülle meiner Illusion.

اینجا و آنجا

مرزی ست شفاف
در برابر چشمانم
میان اینجا و آنجا
که ناهماهنگی شان
آشکارمی کند برایم رازی را

اینجا و آنجا
همگام
پنهان در وجودم
چون شکافی در قلبم

و این شفافیت است
که با آغوشی باز
می گذارد خود آستانی شوم
میان اینجا و آنجا
آماده برای رسیدن به باوری
برای درهم شکستن
پوسته نازک پندارم.

Sehnsucht

Sehnsucht nach des Flusses Strömung,
lässt verbinden
die Herzenswörter zum Echo
des wahrhaftig Ganzen.
Das Echo,
so bedeutend,
so erfüllend,
als würde der Duft
meines Liebsten mich umgeben,
wo ich schließlich befreit
mich hingeben dem Kusse
der aufsteigenden Morgensonne.

آرزو

آرزوی همسو شدن
با تلاطم دریا
بازتاب آوای قلب
به حقیقت زندگی ست

این آوا
چه پر معنا
چه سرشار
چون هاله ای ست
از بوی خوش آنکه دوستش دارم
آنگاه رها شده
تسلیم بوسه طلوع خورشید
می شوم.

Jutta Lehmann
Germany

Fragt nicht

Fragt nicht –
Ihr müsst mein Leben
nicht verstehen
ich kann es selber kaum

Wie ich in manchen
schweren Stunden
gerettet wurde
tausendfach
dass mich gehalten
eine Kraft
die nicht
mein eigen war
und mich getragen
sonderbar
ja, oftmals
gegen meinen Willen
als wüsste ein Anderer
den besseren Weg
den er für mich
erwählt zu gehen
von Anfang an

Er ließ mich
meine Freiheit kosten
doch fing mich auf
am Scheideweg:

Ich habe dich je geliebt.

نپرسید چرا

نپرسید چرا
زندگی من اینگونه است
من خود پاسخی ندارم
که چگونه از لحظات سخت زندگی گذشتم

هزاران بار جان به در بردم
بدون آن که خود بدانم
به طرز شگفتی نجات یافتم
آری، بارها
حتی بدون آنکه خود بخواهم
گویی که او می دانست
که چه راهی را باید رفت
راهی که او برایم برگزیده بود

از همان ابتدا با اینکه
در انتخاب خود آزاد بودم
همیشه مرا بر سر دو راهی
یاری کرد

همیشه دوستت داشتم.

Wenn ich die Stille zulasse

Wenn ich die Stille
zulasse
sprechen tausend Stimmen –
die einzige schweigt
verschlossen im Tresor
des Unsagbaren
bewahrt sie
ihr Geheimnis
im Schweigen
der Ewigkeit.

اگر خاموشی پیشه کنم

اگر خاموشی پیشه کنم
هزاران صدا سخن می گویند

تنها یک صدا
درون صندوقچه ناگفته ها
با سکوت
راز خود را
در خاموشی ابدی
پاس می دارد.

Helene Levar
Austria

Gebet zum Schutzengel

Bleib bei mir, bis sich des Tages Last zu Ende neigt,
und die Hektik langer Stunden schweigt.

Bleib bei mir, bis all der Lärm verklingt,
und die Nachtigall ihr Liedchen singt.

Bleib bei mir, bis alles dunkel wird,
und die Nacht die ruhige Zeit gebiert.

Bleib bei mir, wenn meine Hast zu Ende geht,
und der gute Mond am Himmel steht.

Bleib bei mir, wenn schöne Träume kommen,
durch die ich neue Kraft gewonnen.

Bleib bei mir, wenn die Erinnerung mich quält,
sage mir, dass nur das Heute zählt.

Steh mir bei, wenn dann die Todesglocke läutet,
was ew'gen Frieden wohl bedeutet.

Geh mit mir und gib mir Deine Hand,
bei der Reise ins jenseitige Land.

نیایشی با فرشته نجات

با من بمان تا پایان سنگینی روز
و رسیدن آرامش
پس از ساعات طولانی پرهیاهو

با من بمان تا خاموشی هر صدایی
و شنیدن نغمه بلبل

با من بمان به هنگام چیرگی تاریکی
بر روز
و رسیدن آرامش شب

با من بمان تا پایان بیتابی ام
و پدیدار شدن ماه تابان
در آسمان

با من بمان تا رسیدن رویاهای زیبا
و جان تازه گرفتن از زندگی

با من بمان
به هنگام یادآوری خاطرات تلخ
و به من بگو
تنها امروز
را باید زیست

در کنار من بمان
آنگاه که صدای ناقوس مرگ
نشانه آرامش ابدی است

با من بیا
و دستت را به من بده
هنگام سفر به سوی ابدیت.

Erwin Matl
Austria

Veränderung

Beschwerlich genug waren sie
die langen Wintermonate
doch schmerzhaft auch
unsere frostigen Beziehungen
im Berufsleben, im Alltagstrott
innerhalb unserer Familien,
im Kleinen und im Großen

Nach dem Winterschlaf
kündigt sich das Sprießen
neuer Knospen an
das Licht wärmender Sonne
kann auch uns
aus unserer Dunkelheit
und Hoffnungslosigkeit
herausführen

Das Erwachen der Natur
eine Chance zum Neubeginn
unserer menschlichen Begegnungen
der Gewöhnlichkeit unseres Alltags
der Ungewissheit des Suchens
der Spannungen des Lebens
unserer Entscheidungen
in der Wärme der Maiensonne

Beschwerlich genug
waren sie
die langen Wintermonate.

دگرگونی

چه دشوار
شب های طولانی زمستانی
و چه دردناک
یخ زدگی روابط انسانی
در همه ساحت های زندگی
از کوچک و بزرگ

جوانه های نورس
می شکفند
پس از خواب زمستانی
و نور گرم خورشید
رهایی ست
از سیاهی و ناامیدی

با بیداری زندگی
مجالی برای تولدی دیگر
دید و بازدیدها
و خو گرفتن
به روزمَرُّه گی
در خروش
و تلاطم زندگی
زیر آفتاب دلچسب بهاری

چه دشوار
شکیبایی شب های طولانی زمستانی.

Sonnenstrahlen

Über Nacht
ist es wärmer geworden
überraschend sind
die ersten Knospen
aufgesprungen,
ein wunderbarer
Blüten-Teppich
liegt über Feld und Land.

Neue Energie
durchströmt uns,
gibt der Frische
des Morgens
eine wohlgeformte
neue Richtung.

Nichts
in unserem Leben
ist Zufall,
Zuversicht
bestimmt den
Lauf unserer
Tage.

Ich danke
dem himmlischen Vater
für den neuen Frühling
mit Dir.

آفتاب

گرم شدن نابهنگام هوا
شکفتن اولین غنچه ها
پهن شدن شگفت انگیز فرشِ گل
بر روی زمین و کشتزارها
می افروزد نور امیدی در دلِ ما
به طراوتِ صبحِ نوین

در زندگی هیچ رویدادی
نابهنگام نیست
باور به نیکبختی
آرمان زندگی است

سپاس از خالق هستی
برای فرارسیدن بهاری دیگر
با تو.

Sylvia Meise
Germany

Aufstehn

Als der Tag Tag war
und die Nacht sein Brunnen.
Als die Brust Brust war
und die Zunge rosa und rau.

Als der Süden noch nicht geboren war
der große, trockene Süden.
Als der Norden noch der
Spiegel der Sonne war
und ewiges Weiß
waren die Menschen noch jung
doch die Angst war schon da.

Begann zu glüh'n
erkaltete in der Schönheit
unserer Waffen
die Armbrust der Macht
blendet seither die Sonne
bricht Eos die Finger
brennt Angst zu Asche
in den Sperrfeuern der Nacht.

Doch
noch immer
gilt Aufsteh'n als Zeichen
Tag für Tag
Jetzt du!

برپا خیز

آنگاه که روز
روز بود
و شب چشمه روز

آنگاه که سینه
سینه بود
و زبان زبر و صورتی رنگ

آنگاه که جنوبِ خشک و وسیع
هنوز زاده نشده بود
و شمال هنوز آینه‌ی خورشید
و روشنی جاودانه بود
و انسان‌ها
هنوز بدون لکه گناه

ترس اما
از دیرگاه وجود داشت
که در زیبایی سرد سلاح هایمان
در تیر و کمان خشونت
شعله ور می شد

تا این که روی خورشید تیره شد
و انگشتِ اِئوس[11] شکست
و خاکستر ترس
در آتش سوزی های شبانه سوخت

اما طلوع یک روز نو
نشانه رستاخیز است
و اکنون نوبت توست
برپا خیز.

---

[11] اِئوس Eos، الهه‌ی سپیده دم در اساطیر یونانی.

Boris Pfeiffer
Germany

Dir zuzuhören ist manchmal,
als sähe ich dem Sonnenaufgang zu.
Deine Stimme kommt in den Tag,
beginnt ihn. Dein Herzschlag
verkündet, dass etwas weitergeht.
Und da liegt eine Schläfrigkeit
zwischen deinen Stimmbändern,
die, wenn ich an sie denke, keine
Fragen in mir zurücklässt.

گوش سپردن به **تو**
چون تماشای
طلوع خورشیدست
روز با نوای تو آغاز می شود
و صدای ضربان قلبت
نشانه ادامه زندگی ست

حتی فکر خستگی صدای تو
هیچ یک از سئوالات مرا
بی پاسخ نمی گذارد.

Ich male dir Herzschläge
in die Nacht, tiefe und
ruhige. Solange,
so viele, bis du das
nächste Mal aufwachst
und es wieder machst:
mmmmmmmmmm...

Dann raschelnde
pfotenhafte, solche von
Regen auf Blattwerk,
atemlose und wieder
tiefe lange.

Geflüster deines
Namens in mir,
Nebel, der sich zum
kommenden Morgen
ballt, um die

Schönheit der Sonne
vor dir auszubreiten

در امتداد شب
تپش آرام و ژرف قلبت را
بارها و بارها می نگارم
تا از خواب برخیزی
و دوباره زمزمه کنی:
امممممم...

آنگاه برایت
آهنگ بارش باران
روی شاخ و برگ را
نفس زنان
همراه تپش آرام و ژرف قلبت
می نگارم

زمزمه نام تو در من
مانند مِه یی ست در صبحگاهان
که با محو خود
زیبایی خورشید را
در برابر روی تو آشکار می کند.

Ich möchte dich mit Herbstlaub bedecken,
dann bist du bunt wie der ganze Wald.
Ich möchte dich küssen
und blaue Flüsse in dir wecken,
mit denen du mich umarmst.

می خواهم بپوشانم
پیکرت را با برگ های پاییزی
تا رنگارنگ شوی
چون تمامی جنگل
می خواهم ببوسمت
و بیدار کنم رودهای
آبی رنگ وجودت را
تا مرا با آب آن
در آغوش گیری.

Nasrin Siege
Iran/Germany

Heimatlos

Der Heimatlose ist ein Reisender,
der in fremden Hotels aus dem Koffer lebt,
an neuen Stränden nach Muscheln sucht
und in den Gesichtern das Vertraute,
das Lächeln.

وطنْ آواره

وطنْ آواره
مسافری ست
با همه زندگی ا ش
در یک چمدان
در هتل های ناشناس
در سواحل بیگانه
به دنبال صدفی
و چهره ای
با لبخندی آشنا.

Kuss des Augenblicks

Mein Begleiter
Mein Traum
Leicht
So leicht
Der Kuss
Des Augenblicks
Die Berührung so zart
Doch bald
Erinnerung nur
Und Dunkelheit am Tag

بوسه یک دم

همدمِ من
رویایم
سبک
نرم
لمس ملایمِ بوسه
یک دم

یادش تنها
خاطره ای
چون تاریکی در روز.

Da sein

Da sein ist nicht
hier sein
und doch drängen sie sich
auf
die persischen Worte
wollen gesprochen
gehört werden
die Bilder
des Vergangenen
benennen.

Verschämt
so linkisch
das Kind
das sie einst
besaß
sie sagen will
sie hören will
doch nicht mehr kann
auf der Zunge
vertraut doch stumm
das Ungesagte...

بودن در این مکان

بودن در این مکان
به معنی در اینجا بودن نیست
هجوم واژه های فارسی
که می خواهند بر زبان آورده
و شنیده شوند
و بازگو کنند
تصاویر گذشته را

خجلت زده
و فرومانده
چون کودکی که روزی
این زبان، زبان او بود
می خواهد به سخن آید
و بشنود این واژه ها را

اما دیگر
توان به زبان آوردن
این کلمات آشنا را ندارد
و ناگفته ها
خاموش مانده بر زبان.

Antje Stehn
Germany

Holocaust Gedenktag

Schlüsselbegriff:
Vergangenheitsbewältigung oder - Aufarbeitung?
Und der ästhetische Diskurs?
Hält ein Gedicht der Barbarei stand?
Menschliche Sprache eine tröstende Überdecke
oder ein Zahnschmerz der bis in die Wurzeln geht
wo immerhin wir uns begeben dasselbe Pattern
eingepflanzt wie ein Mikrochip unter die Haut
Selbstaufwertung durch Abwertung anderer
gibt es ein Danach
solange die Erinnerung das heute nicht einschließt?

روز یادبود هولوکاست

اصلاحِ کلیدی:
توجیه گذشته یا - روشنگری؟
یا گفتمانی توخالی
برای نمایش واژگونه توحش انسانی؟

آیا شعر توان توصیف بربریت را دارد؟
آیا زبان انسانی وسیله ای ست
برای پوشاندن تبهکاری و آرام کردن افکار
یا مانند دندانی ست
که درد آن نشانه ی رنجِ انسانی ست؟

انسان هایی ماشینی
با میکروچیپ کاشته شده زیر پوست
همگی به یک شکل
خودشیفتگی
با پَست کردن دیگران
آیا بَعدی هم وجود خواهد داشت
تا زمانی که حافظه
امروز را نادیده می گیرد؟

Wo Sinnfetzen finden
in diesem ständigen Gewirr
können wir noch wie eine Kletterpflanze
tastend denken
schlängelnd hinwachsen
zu Mitmenschen, zur Gemeinschaft
zur Menschheit?
Unser Garten war vor uns da
vor dem Aussäen
vor dem Ordnen der Pflänzchen in Reihen
vor dem Trennen der Gesunden von den Kranken
Jetzt drängen alle in verschiedene Richtungen
rivalisieren statt
sich zu verknüpfen im Ganzen
ein jeder ruft nach Frieden
aus seiner eigenen Ecke
Gedanken im Singular
sind kein Privileg
der Garten war
für das Zusammen
gedacht

در این آشفته بازار
با افکار از هم گسیخته
آیا می توانیم مانند گیاهان رونده
آهسته بِروییم؟

آیا می توانیم با تأمل فکر کرده
و در پیچ و خم زندگی
در کنار یکدیگر
با انسانیت رشد و نُمِو کنیم؟

این باغ زندگی
این زمین
برای همه ما خلق شده
قبل از اینکه به زمین کشاورزی بدل شود
قبل از کاشتن گیاهان
به دست ما
قبل از دستچین کردن انسان ها
و جدا کردن نا توانان از توانمندان

با چشم و همچشمی
بجای همبستگی و همراهی در زندگی
هر یک از ما تنها در گوشه ای
با فریاد آرزوی رسیدن به صلح
سر درگم

فکر کردن در تنهایی
برای ما امتیازی نیست

زمین ما
این باغ زندگی
برای همه ما خلق شده.

Peter Völker
Germany

Verflossene Jahreszeiten

Sommer war's
als ich lieben lernte,
heißer Wind
blies mir entgegen,
streichelte mich
bis zum Herbst.
Dieser eine Herbst
war verflucht bunt.
Im Winter fror ich,
wie jedes Jahr
in meiner Schreibkammer.
Nur deine Worte wärmten mich
in diesem deutschen Winter.
Schnee stob gegen mein Fenster.
Den Frühling rief, ersehnte ich,
so sehr - unseren Frühling.
Aber er kam und kam nicht,
blieb draußen in der Ferne,
aus unserem Leben.
Wir warteten viele Jahre
 auf unseren Frühling,
und wurden dabei alt.

سال های از دست رفته

تابستان بود که عشق را آموختم
نسیمی آتشین به سوی من وزید
و مرا تا آمدن پاییز نوازش کرد
و این بار پاییز چه زیبا
و رنگارنگ بود

هنگامی که برف
به پنجره اتاقم می کوبید
در این زمستان سرد آلمان
پشت میز کارم یخ بستم
تنها یاد تو و واژگان تو
مرا گرما می بخشید

تا بهار از راه رسید
و افسوس از آرزوی رسیدنِ بهار ما
که نرسید و نرسید
و در دوردست ها گم شد

دیریست
در آرزوی رسیدنِ بهارمان
پیر شدیم.

Spuren der Erlösung

Ermattet die
Flügelschläge
Deiner Zeit

Zwischen deinen
Lebensfedern
Sonne und Sturm

Sorgenspuren
In deinem Gesicht
Im Seelengrund
Geglättet nun

Gedanken an dich
Gefühle für dich
Leben fort
In meiner Trauer

Eine Südbrise
Vom fernen Meer
Weht dich fort
Geliebte Seele

Du und ich erlöst
Nicht gelöst
Verbunden

به یاد لیلی

نشان رستگاری

چه بیرنگ شد
پرواز شتابابگونه دوران بودنَت

خورشید و طوفان
در برگ برگِ زندگی ات

فرونشست چروک نگرانی
در سیما
و ژرفای جان تو

در سوگ تو
و در خیال
و حسِ با تو بودن
روان در بستر جاری زندگی

در دوردست ها
نسیمی جان باشکوه تو را
با خود می بَرَد

رستگاری تو،
رهایی توست
نه جدایی تو از من

من و تو یکی شدیم
جاودانه
یگانه.

Mária Bátorová
Slovakia

BRIEŽDENIE

Vo výške
korún stromov
rastú vo februári
ako každý rok
pred jarou

Hniezda

Konárik na konárik
zobáčiky
stavajú
pevné
bývanie
pre nový život

Len láska a harmónia
v sne o budúcnosti
sa takto namáha
s láskou čaká
v obetiach
život

Večerné zore
mení na ranné

Dämmerung

In der Höhe
der Kronen der Bäume
wachsen im Februar
wie jedes Jahr
im Vor-Frühling
Nester

Zweig um Zweig
bereiten
zarte tüchtige Schnäbel
festes
fabelhaftes Wohnen
für neues Leben

Nur Liebe und Harmonie
können
im Zukunftstraum
durch Emsigkeit
und Opferbereitschaft
Leben ermöglichen

Ja, sogar die Abenddämmerung
zur Morgendämmerung
verwandeln.

غروب

مثل هر سال پیش از بهار
در ماه فوریه
پرندگان
لانه می سازند
روی تاج درختان
برای یک زندگی نوین

با منقارهای ظریف
تَرکه تَرکه می سازند
لانه ای افسانه ای

تنها با عشق و همیاری
می توان ساخت
رویای آینده را
با تلاش و کوشش
و فداکاری

آنگاه حتی غروب
سپیده دم می شود.

Do ulíc bedárov

Do ulíc bedárov
Vychádzam
V čiernom
Čierne sú úsmevy
Čiernych sestier
Čierne myšlienky
Na čierno snežia
Do ulíc

Čierňavu bedárov
So sebou vlečiem

Čierne sú svedomia
Figúrok v parlamente
Čierny čas pokánia
Tu trvá večne

Pane!
Na tomto kúsku
Zeme
Čas vzkriesenia
Nenastane?

In die Straßen der Elenden hinaus

In die Straßen der Elenden hinaus
gehe ich
schwarz gekleidet
Schwarz das Lächeln
der schwarzen Schwestern
Schwarze Gedanken
schneien schwarz
in die Straßen

Die Schwärze der Elenden
schleppe ich mit mir
Schwarz das Gewissen
der Marionetten im Parlament
die schwarze Zeit der Buße
wird hier ewig dauern

O, Herr!
Wird wohl
auch auf diesem Fleckchen Erde
die Auferstehung
jemals geschehen?

در امتداد کوچه شوربختی

در امتداد کوچه شوربختی
با لباس سیاه
قدم می زنم
لبخند خواهرانم سیاه
با افکار سیاه
می بارد در کف خیابان ها
برف سیاه

شوربختی سیاهی
را با خود به دنبال می کشم
با وجدان سیاه مسئولین سرسپرده کشورم
و کفاره این دوره سیاهی که در این شهر
گویی تا ابد ادامه خواهد داشت

خدایا
آیا رستاخیزی در این نقطه
از زمین به پا خواهد شد؟

Soledad Benages Amorós
Spain

POESÍA, esa arma

No hemos perdido la esperanza.
El poema es la voz que aplasta
la estulticia de los traficantes de esclavos.

Acorralemos con la humildad del verso
la arrogancia del carroñero.
Avivemos con la inmensidad del poema
la fuerza del fuego nunca destruido,
la llama diminuta o la hoguera gigante
que nadie
        logró
                apagar
                        nunca.

Hay millones de instantes de poesía en el planeta.
Hay millones de voces en el cosmos
que resuenan cada vez que dos o más poetas sonríen
y lanzan su voz para la esperanza o
su grito de indignación para la lucha.

Habrá muchos amaneceres
que traerán sueños y complicidades.

Prosigue, poeta, el canto de alborada:
"La vida surgirá de la oscuridad de las raíces"
en un otoño tornasolado.

Poetry, that weapon

We haven't given up hope.
The poem is the voice that crushes
the foolishness of the sunrise traffickers.

Let us corner with the humility of the verse
the arrogance of the scavenger.
Let's relive with the immensity of the poem
the force of fire never destroyed,
the tiny flame or the giant bonfire
that nobody achieved turn off never.

There are millions of moments of poetry on the planet.
There are millions of echoes in the cosmos
that resonate every time two or more poets
smile and cast their voice for hope
or their cry of indignation for the struggle.

There will be many sunrises
that bring dreams and complicity.

Pursue, poet, the song of dawn:
Life will emerge from the darkness of the roots
in this twilight autumn.

شعر چون سلاح

ما امیدمان را از دست ندادیم
شعر ندایی ست
برای رسواییِ حماقتِ تاجرانِ طلوعِ خورشید

بیایید با فروتنیِ شعر
تکبّرِ این غارتگران را
درهم شکنیم
بیایید با شکوهِ شعر
دوباره بیَفروزیم
شعله آتشی را
که هرگز خاموش نمی شود

در سیاره ما
لحظه های بی شماری وجود دارد
که خود نشانی از
شعر است
با لبخند و آوای هر شاعری
پژواک صدایشان را
در کهکشان می شنویم
که نشانه امید یا فریاد مبارزه آنهاست

طلوع خورشیدهای بسیار
در راه است
که رویای همبستگی را
به ارمغان می آورد

رهرو شاعری باش
که نغمه طلوع سپیده دم را
نوید می دهد:
آنگاه زندگی
در گرگ و میش این پاییز

از درون تاریکخانه ریشه ها پدیدار می شود.

EPICENTRO DE LA SOLEDAD

> *Prendida de tu ausencia mi mirada,*
> *contra todo me doy, ciego me hiero*
> *Me he quedado sin pulso*
> *Ángel González.*

No hay lumbre que pueda prender
en mi corazón.

Ni el agua del jazmín
puede perfumar el recóndito silencio.

Si existen flores,
son clandestinas.

El delito: la utopía.

Siempre el amor adentro
por el laberinto inacabable
del deseo
– ¡oh, sueño robado!-

Sola,
en el instante de espinas para la tristeza.

Una mirada absorta en lo infinito
desde el epicentro de la soledad.

Epicentre of the loneliness

There is no flame that can ignite
in my heart.

Neither the jasmine water
can perfume
the hidden silence.

If there are flowers,
are clandestine.

The crime: the utopia.

Love always going inside
through the endless labyrinth
of desire
- Oh, stolen dream!

Alone,
in the moment of thorns for sadness.

A look lost in the infinite
from the epicentre of loneliness.

در ژرفای تنهایی

هیچ شعله ای نمی تواند
قلب مرا روشن کند

هیچ عصاره یاسی نمی تواند
سکوت پنهان را معطر کند

اگر گلی هست
پنهان است

جُرم ما
آرمان گرایی ماست

اما عشق همواره در درون ما
در میان پیچ و خمِ بی انتهای آرزویی ست

- آه این آرزوی گمشده
تنها بر خار درد و رنج نگاهی ست
گمشده در بی نهایت
در ژرفای تنهایی.

Giovanna Benedetti
Panama/Spain

Pabellón de la rosa

A rose is a rose is a rose is a rose...
Gertrude Stein

Detrás de todo resplandor está la rosa.
En una sombra fugaz, también lo está.
Moviéndose silenciosa, en la nostalgia, está la rosa,
y está en el fondo del mar y en las promesas.

Hay una rosa invisible dando la vuelta al viento
y una rosa atrevida por cada robo de un beso.
Hay una rosa desnuda, en la noche, bailando
y una nube de rosas cuando cae el aguacero.

Rosas hay que son santuarios de sombras peregrinas.
Rosas hay que abren sus párpados en lo infinito de un sueño.
Rosas ha de haber eternas bajo un balcón que espera
y no han de faltar rosas a aquellos que nos dejan.

Una rosa es ya cristal si la traen los recuerdos
pero es rosa primordial si se la pinta al lienzo.
Y es que el arte, en su mensura, es una fuerza de rosas
y no hay rosa imposible cuando se escribe un poema.

Hay rosas impasibles, tutelares, lisonjeras
(O rosas abismales, como esa de la guerra).
Hay rosas que son números, y rosas que son letras
porque la rosa es la rosa... es la rosa... es la rosa.

Pavilion of the rose

A rose is a rose is a rose is a rose...
Gertrude Stein

Behind every glow
there is a rose.
In a fleeting shadow, it is too.
Moving quietly, in nostalgia,
there is also a rose,
and it is at the bottom of the sea
and in all promises.

There is an invisible rose
turning around in the wind.
And a daring rose
for each theft of a kiss.
There is a naked rose, dancing,
at the middle of the night,
and a cloud of roses
when the downpour falls.

There are roses
that are shrines of pilgrim shadows.
There are roses
that open their eyelids
in the infinity of a dream.
There must be eternal roses
under a balcony waiting
and there's no shortage of roses
to those who leave us.

A rose is already crystal
if it is brought by memories
but it is primordial rose
if it is painted on the canvas.
And it's just that art
In his measurement it's a force of roses
and there is no impossible rose
when writing a poem.
There are impassive,
flatteting and tutelary roses,
(or abysmal roses, like that of the war).

There are roses that are numbers
and roses that are letters
because the rose
is the rose, is the rose...
it's the rose.

"یک گل رُز، گل رُز است. رُز، رُز"
Gertrud Stein

گلستانی از گل رُز

در فراسوی هر اخگری
گل رُزی ست
در سایه ا ی گریزان
با حرکتی آرام
در نوستالوژی، بر بستر دریاها
و در همه وعده ها

در پنهان نیز
رُزی در آغوش باد
می رقصد
رُزی بی باک
برای بوسه ها ی پنهانی

رُز برهنه ای هم
در نیمه های شب می رقصد
و ابری از رُز
هنگامی که باران می بارد

و رُزی در زیارتگاهِ سایه زائران
رُزهایی که پلک هایشان را
در بینهایت رویای خود باز می کنند

و رُزهای جاودان منتظری زیر بالکن
رُزهایی که می میرند
می روید
جایشان رُزهای دیگری

رُزی که
در یاد ما زنده است

رُزی ست از کریستال
گل رُزی راستین
که روی بوم نقاشی رسم می شود
و این همان سرشت زیبای رُز است

در بیان شعر
هیچ گل رُزی دروغین نیست

رُز سرد و بی احساس
رُزی مخوف
مانند رُزی
در پرتگاه جنگ
و همچنین رُز خوب و مهربان

رُزهایی هستند
که سمبل اعدادند
رُزهایی از حروف الفبا
چرا که رُز، یک گل رُز است
رُز، رُز
و این همان گل رُز است.

Pensar desde la nada

                Le cedo
la mirada a la palabra
—en el doble sentido de la voz y el término—
y me doy al ejercicio de pensar desde la nada
mientras la madrugada toma la forma
de una larga playa oscura
que desafía las advertencias
de la claridad que avanza.
                Le cedo
la palabra a la mirada
—allí donde la uña aún no sale del zarpazo—
la luz no florecida sigue esperando el gesto
en lo que va del titubeo
al salto inevitable.

Everything from nothing

I yield my eyes before the word
(In the double understanding
of its voice and meaning)
and entertain myself in thinking
in everything that comes from nothing
while the early morning comes
to take its shape
before all sounds
like a dark and empty seashore
that defies all warnings
of the light that advances.

I yield the word before my eyes
(in that insidous moment when the nail
has still dont come out of the paw)
and the unflowered light
is still waiting for the body
so far from hesitation
towards the inevitable jump.

هستی از درون نیستی

چشم هایم
به سوی کلمه ای خیره می شود
با حسِ آهنگ و معنی آن
و با این فکر
که همه چیز از نیستی آغاز می شود

هنگامی که
صبح آغاز می شود
تا در قالب روز ظاهر شود
قبل از آنکه صدایی
به گوش رسد
چون ساحلی تیره و خالی ست
که در مسیر پرپیچ و خم خود
به روشنایی نوری نزدیک می شود

این بار کلمه را
در برابر چشمانم می گیرم
در این لحظه شگفت انگیز
که ناخن ها
هنوز از پنجه بیرون نزده اند
و روشنی هنوز زاییده نشده
چرا که او
درانتظار ظهور کالبدی ست
که بی درنگ
با پرشی ناگزیر
با او درآمیزد.

Antonio Capilla Loma
Spain

BEBÍ EL GRIAL DE LA ILUSIÓN PERDIDA

Bebí el grial de la ilusión perdida
el despertar de la inocencia al mundo
el sufrimiento azul de ser consciente
el resistir mientras nos traga el barro.

Sentí la voz que grita en el vacío
en la oquedad donde la voz se quiebra
en la silueta que al amor escapa
en el silencio de un sepulcro abierto.

Hundí las manos en la tierra estéril
regué la flor de la piedad filial
la sangre fértil de una llaga inmensa
el vino amargo del doliente cáliz.

Yo he recreado la palabra diáfana
el centro mismo en que el latido es vida
la hondura excelsa que a la cumbre accede
claror de sombras en el verso franco.

Y pido al fin que me perdonen todos
por ver la luz cuando la noche cae
por ser feliz cuando mi hermano sufre
por existir cuando las voces mueren.

I Drank The Grail Of Lost Dreams

I drank the grail of lost dreams
the awakening of innocence to the world
the blue suffering of being conscious
the resistance to being swallowed by the mud.

I sank my hands into the barren land
I watered the flower of filial piety
the fertile blood of an immense wound
the bitter wine of the suffering chalice.

I heard the voice that screams in the void
in the hollow where the voice breaks
in the silhouette that flees to love
in the sublime depth that reaches the summit
in the clearness of shadows in the frank verse.

I have recreated the diaphanous word
the very heart where a beat means life
the sublime depth that reaches the summit
the brightness of shadows in the honest verse.

And I finally beg for forgiveness from all
for seeing the light when night falls
for being happy when my brother suffers
for existing when voices die.

از جامِ رویاهای گمشده نوشیدم

از جامِ رویاهای گمشده نوشیدم
بیداری معصوم جهان را
رنجِ درک و آگاهی را
وحشت بلعیده شدن در باتلاق را

دستانم را
در سرزمین خشک و بی حاصل
فرو بردم
و گُلِ پاکِ دوران کودکی ام را
آبیاری کردم
با خون ریخته شده
از یک زخم کهنه
و شراب تلخِ جامِ رنج

پژواک فریادی تهی را
در غاری شنیدم
در افقی که به سوی عشق می گریزد
در ژرفای عمیقی که
به فراز قله ای می رسد
در سایه روشن شعری ناتمام

و در پایان
خواستار بخشش شما هستم
چون با دیدن شب
آمدن روز را می بینم
با دیدن رنجِ انسان
باز قادر هستم که
خوشبخت باشم
و وقتی صدایی می میرد
باز زنده ام.

EL MURO

Cuando sientes que el muro está blindado
que no hay puerta de entrada ni salida
que el miedo y el dolor te paralizan
te clavan a la angustia
lloras.
Pero el muro se queda
forjado por el odio
y el miedo con tus ojos
se hacen uno en el llanto.
Entonces, gritas.
Pero el muro no quiebra
permanece inmutable
y el dolor con tus labios
se hacen uno en el grito.
Entonces, cantas.
Y el canto es grito es llanto y es canción
y salta el muro y vuela y se ilumina
y es luz que nos señala y nos revela
que a este lado del muro el dado
está en el aire.

The Wall

When you feel that the wall is armored
that there is no entrance or exit
that fear and pain paralyze you
they nail you to anguish

you cry

but the wall remains
forged by hate
and the fear with your eyes
they become one in the cry

then you scream

but the wall does not break
remains undaunted
and the pain with your lips
they become one in the scream
then you sing

and the song is a scream is a cry and is a song
and jump the wall and fly and lights up
and it is light that points us and reveals us
that on this side of the wall

the dice is in the air.

دیوار

اگر در برابرت دیوارِ پولادینی می بینی

که هیچ راه ورود و خروجی ندارد

و دردت تو را فلج کرده

و در درون

رنج میخکوبت می کند

فریادی برمی کشی

ولی این دیوار نفرت

همچنان پابرجاست

و ترس در چشمان تو

با فریادت

یکی می شود

اما این دیوار

با همه بی شرمی

پابرجاست

و تَرَک برنمی دارد

این درد

با لب های تو

در فریادت یکی می شود

آنگاه که تو می خوانی

و شعر تو اشکی می شود

فریادی و آهنگی

شعر تو، پروازکنان

از دیوار عبور می کند

و نور می شود

این نور

با روشنی خود

به ما نشان می د هد

بخت ما

در آن سوی دیوار است.

Metin Cengiz
Turkey

GÜL

Şu imgemdeki biçimli bahçen
Gidip gelemediğim geçmiş gibi
Orada hep öyle güzel açacak
Sonsuzluk içinde açacak
İmgemdeki o bahçe

Rose

Your shapely garden in that image of mine
Like the past I plunged into, never to return
Will always blossom so beautifully there
Will blossom eternally there
The garden in that image of mine

Translated to English by Neil O Doherty

گل رُز

باغ زیبای تو در خیال من
چون گذشته ای ست
که نمی توان به آن پا نهاد
و دوباره بازگشت
آنجا اما
همچنان می ماند
شکوفا.

در خیال من
این باغ
می ماند شکوفا
تا ابد.

ZAMANIN SÖYLETTİĞİ

Sümüklüböcek gibi İz
Bırakarak kuru yapraklar üstünde
Geçiyor zaman içimden
Payımı aldım bu dünyadan
Çamur, zift ve dalgalarla gelen tasa
Bu dünyada yer bırakmıyor aşka
Neyin oğluyum ben-
Karanlık kum gibi kaynıyor etrafımda
Ve güneş ve buzdan bir çöl
Sözcüklerin çatısı çatırdıyor-
Yıkılıyor güvendiğim dağlar
Sanki kuşkudan yapılmış bir oyuğum
Uğulduyor içimdeki rüzgâr

What Time Has Us Say

Like a snail,
On dry leaves leaving trails,
Time slips through me

I have had my share of this world-
The sorrows that come with mud, pitch, and wave,
Leave no place for love.

What then I am the son of-
Around me like sand darkness abounds
And the sun and a desert of ice

The roof of words cracks
The mountains I entrusted collapse
As if I were a cavern made of doubt
The wind inside me howls.

Translated to English by Neil O Doherty

پیامِ زمان

چون رَدِّ پای حلزون
روی برگ خشک
حرکت زمان
حک می شود بر من

من دِین خود را ادا کرده ام
به این دنیا
درد و رنج همراه با گِل و لای امواج
جایی نمی گذارند
برای دوست داشتن

من فرزند که هستم
که به گِردِ من تاریکیِ تام است
و خورشید و صحرایی از یخ ؟

بام واژه ها فرو می ریزند
و کوه های باورم فرومی پاشند
چون غاری از شک و تردیدم
نفس در سینه ام می گرید.

Silvia Cuevas Morales
Chile/ Spain

Volver al hogar

¿Debería retornar una vez más?
¿Volverán a abrirse antiguas heridas?
¿Volverán los recuerdos
a acosarme a toda prisa?
¿Me reconocerán las amistades de mi infancia?
¿Encontraré el antiguo camino a casa?
¿Me esperarán esos cálidos abrazos
con los que he soñado tantas veces?
¿Pasarán ululando las balas cerca de mi cabeza?
¿Seguirá la sangre manchando
las aceras de mi juventud?
¿Los fantasmas de los tanques seguirán arrastrando
sus pesadas cadenas por las aceras?
¿Encontraré puertas abiertas o cerradas?
¿Hallaré un hogar?

Going Back Home

Should I go back again?
Will old wounds reopen once again?
Will memories come rushing back to haunt me?
Will my childhood friends recognize me?
Will I find my old way home?
Will I find the warm embraces
I have so much dreamed of?
Will the bullets whistle past my head?
Will the blood still stain
The footpaths of my youth?
Will the ghosts of thanks continue
To drag their heavy chains down the road?
Will I find open or close doors?
Will I find a home?

بازگشت به وطن

آیا می توانم دوباره به وطنم بازگردم؟
آیا زخم های کهنه دوباره باز نمی شوند؟
آیا خاطراتِ دردناک
باردیگر در جانِ من رخنه نمی کنند؟
آیا اگر دوستانِ دورانِ کودکی ام
مرا نشناسند، ناامید خواهم شد؟
آیا می توانم دوباره راه خانه مان را پیدا کنم؟
آیا وطنم مرا مثل رویاهایم
با آغوش گرم پذیرا می شود؟
آیا از بالای سرم
گلوله ای شلیک خواهد شد؟
آیا جای پای جوانی ام
هنوز آغشته به خون خواهد بود؟
آیا هنوز ماشین های جنگی سنگین
از خیابان ها عبور می کنند؟
آیا کسی درِ خانه اش را
به روی من خواهد گشود؟
آیا باردیگر
میهنِ خویش را بازخواهم یافت؟

11 de septiembre de 1973

Yo vi
Buitres lanzando bombas sobre la Moneda
mancillando la ilusión del pueblo
ensangrentando las alamedas

Yo vi
Títeres disfrazados de falsas primaveras
apostados en los tejados
disparando sobre el pueblo que corría por las aceras

Yo vi
A mi padre pedaleando en una bicicleta rota
camino a casa con el corazón destrozado
como el de sus compañeros en la derrota

Yo vi
A mi madre en lágrimas cosiendo a escondidas
para seguir manteniéndonos
con algunas de sus clientas
    exiliadas
             desaparecidas

Yo escuché
Las ráfagas de madrugada
las botas del enemigo que en cada puerta acechaban
mientras las casas de los traidores
emergían abanderadas

Yo vi
Mi hogar desaparecer en cuatro maletas desvencijadas
    mis amigas
        mis libros
            mi infancia
todo se esfumaba mientras mi país se desangraba

Yo vi
Aquella enorme nave que surcaría los cielos
los ojos llorosos
los pañuelos que se agitaban en el viento
y jamás volví a pisar lo que fue mi pueblo

Yo vi
Y aunque quedara ciega
jamás se borrará el recuerdo
del horror que ese día
hizo su nido en mi pecho

Silvia Cuevas-Morales. Apátrida: Diario de un destierro. Lastura Ediciones, 1ª edición, julio 2017; 2ª edición, octubre de 2018.

September 11th, 1973

I saw
Vultures launching bombs above the Moneda
soiling the hopes of my people
staining tree- lined avenues with blood

I saw
Puppets disguised as false Springs
stationed up on roofs
firing on people running on sidewalks

I saw
My father pedaling a broken bicycle
on his way home, his heart torn
in defeat like those of this fellow worker

I saw
My weeping mother sewing in secret
to continue supporting us
with some of her clients
    exiled
        disappeared

I heard
The burst of gunfire in the early hours
Enemies' boots stalking each door
While from the homes of traitors´
flags emerged

I saw
My home disappears into four rickety suitcases
    my friends
      my books
        my childhood
all vanished while my country bled

I saw
That huge vessel which would plough through the skies
the teary eyes
the handkerchiefs waving in the wind
and I never again stepped on what was my country

I saw
And even if I were blinded
the memory of the horror
that from that day dwells in my soul
will never be erased

---

[12] Moneda is the seat of the president of the Republic of Chile

11 سپتامبر 1973

من شاهد بمباران مونِدا[13]
به خاک سپردن آرزوهای مردم شهرمان
و به خون نشاندن
خیابان های پردرخت مان بودم

من شاهد بودم که چگونه سربازان
بر بامِ خانه ها پنهان شده
و به مردمِ کوچه و خیابان
شلیک می کردند

من شاهد آن بودم
چگونه قلبِ پدرم
که با دوچرخه اش
در راه خانه بود،
پاره پاره شد
و چگونه رفقایش کشته شدند

من شاهد بودم
چگونه مادرم که در خفا
برای ما خیاطی میکرد
تا کمک خرج مان باشد
اشک ریزان با مشتریانش
تبعید و ناپدید شدند

من صبحدمِ یک روز
صدای شلیکِ گلوله ها
و نزدیک شدنِ صدای پوتینِ سربازان
به خانه مان را شنیدم
و شاهد آن بودم
که خائنانی از پنجره ی خانه شان
پرچم سفیدی را
به علامت تسلیم تکان می دادند

من شاهد آن بودم
که چگونه همه زندگی مان
در چهار چمدان جا شد
چگونه همه دوستانم
کتاب هایم و کودکی ام را
درحالیکه کشورم در خون غوطه می خورد
از دست دادم

من شاهد آن بودم
که چگونه بسیاری از هموطنانم، اشک ریزان
در حالیکه دستمال هایشان را
برای خداحافظی در باد تکان می دادند
سوار کشتی بزرگی شدند
که به دوردست ها می رفت
و من هرگز دیگر به آنجایی که
نامش وطن بود
بازنگشتم

آری من شاهد همه این جنایات بودم
که امروز هنوز یادشان
در روح و جانم زنده است
و حتی اگر چشم هایم نمی دید
خاطره آنها هرگز
از یادم پاک نخواهد شد.

---

۱۳ موندا Moneda ، نام کاخ ریاست جمهوری سابق شیلی است.

Maria do Sameiro Barroso
Portugal

Um pássaro atravessando o meu rosto

Sonhos sem fim, o céu roxo,
um pássaro atravessando o meu rosto
– o teu coração uma maravilha –,
o milagre da vida revelando a luz
enquanto vives nos abrigos
do verde, respirando, amando,
trazendo a chuva para dentro de ti.
A terra corrói os esqueletos.
E sobrevives no esplendor
da luz,
nas flores da indigência,
nas estações da fome.
O teu coração é um vale profundo,
verde,
os teus sons são uma peça
musical,
o teu sonho é um pássaro branco,
sumo de romã,
um sussurro de paz.
As tuas mãos são ditosas
percepções da terra.

A Bird Across My Face

Endless dreams, the purple heaven,
a bird across my face
-      your heart a wonder -,
the miracle of life unfolding light
while you live in the shelters
of green, breathing, loving,
bringing the rain inside you.
Earth corrodes skeletons.
And you survive in the splendour
of light,
in the flowers of indigence,
in the stages of hunger.
Your heart is a deep, green
valley,
your sounds are a musical
piece,
your dream is a white bird,
pomegranate juice,
a whisper of peace.
Your hands are blissful
feelings of the earth.

پرنده ای در برابر دیدگانم

رویای بی پایان
آسمان لاجوردی
پرنده ای در برابر دیدگانم

- قلبت شگفت انگیز -
زایش نور، اعجاز هستی
زیرِ چترِ سبزِ زندگی
عشق را دمیدی
و باران را
از درونِ خود زاییدی

آنگاه استخوان ها زیرِ زمین پوسیدند
و تو زیستن را در پناهِ نور
جاودانه کردی
قلبت
ژرفای وادی سبز
بانگت
نوای موسیقی
رویایت
پرنده ای سپید

زمزمه ی سکوت
گنجینه سربسته ای
به سان دانه های آنار

با لمس زمین
زندگی و نشاط را آفریدی.

Junta-me ao teu poema

Junta-me ao teu poema,
junta-me às tuas ilhas,
O sol é ainda um rascunho de cores,
o meu nome é uma noite de luz.

Junta-me aos teus poemas,
junta-me às tuas ilhas,
leva-me desta terra árida.

Doces tâmaraso conduzem-me
das palmeiras do desejo.
Navios verdes conduzem-me
à poção dourada do exílio.

Add me to your poem

Add me to your poem,
join me to your islands,
The sun is still a draft of colours,
my name is a night of brightness.
Add me to your poems,
join me to your islands,
take me from this wasteland.
Sweet dates drive me
from the palm trees of desire.

Green ships drive me
to the golden syrup of exile.

مرا به شعرت اضافه کن

مرا به شعرت اضافه کن
مرا به جزایر وجودت بِبَر
خورشید هنوز نقشی از
رنگ هاست

نام من
شب روشنایی ست

مرا به شعرت اضافه کن
مرا به جزایر وجودت بِبَر
مرا از این برهوت
نجات دِه

خرمای شیرین
مرا به سفر رویایی عاشقانه
می بَرَد

با کشتی سبز رنگ
پناه می بَرَم
به سرزمین طلایی انگبین ها.

Hasan Erkek
Turkey

BOYALI KUŞLAR

İki boyalı kuştuk
boyasız kuşların elinden
ayrı mutsuzluk kadehlerinden içmiştik

İki boyalı kuştuk
vurup kederlerimizi birbirine
şarabi bir düşte seviştik

İki boyalı kuştuk
zaman dışı sayılan
anlık bir mutluluğun üzerine üşüştük

İki boyalı kuştuk
renkleri birbirini tutmayan
ayrı maviliklere uçtuk

Painted Birds

We were two painted birds
drinking from separate glasses of misery
handed to us by birds that had never known paint

We were two painted birds
clinking our sorrows with one another
making love in wine-tinted dreams

We were two painted birds
deemed timeless
we flocked up above a fleeting happiness

We were two painted birds
with colours that failed to match
away we flew to separate blues

Translated to English by Numan Kılıç and Jonathan Ross

پرنده های رنگ شده

ما دو پرنده رنگ شده هستیم
که از پیاله درد و رنجمان
آب می نوشیم
پیاله ای که دیگر پرندگان به ما دادند
پرندگانی که هیچ رنگ دیگری را
نمی شناختند

ما دو پرنده رنگ شده هستیم
که به درد و رنج خود می خندیم
و با رویای رنگ سرخ شراب
به یکدیگر عشق می ورزیم

ما دو پرنده رنگ شده هستیم
که در هر زمان با هر شادی زودگذری
احساس خوشبختی می کنیم

ما دو پرنده رنگ شده هستیم
با رنگ های متفاوت پَر کشیده
و هر یک به سویی پرواز می کنیم.

Sevdadan Kanadım

yumuşak yapraklarında uyuyakaldım
rüyamda ruhumu bir dikişte içtin
kabaran kabuklarına uyandım

ikimize bitimsiz bir bahçe adadım
kirpiklerinle çiçekleri biçtin
kurumuş köklere kaldım

birlikte bir deniz büyüttüğümüzü sandım
suları eteklerinde sürükleyip çektin
beyazlığını yitiren köpüklere bulandım

aysız gecelerde gözlerinde bir yıldız aradım
keskin sözlerinle ince yerlerime mil çekmeyi seçtin
kalbimdeki kırıkları saflığımın tırmığıyla topladım

ve işte şimdi sevdadan kanadım
sen zaten çoktan benden geçtin
artık ben de sana kapandım

şiire açıldım

The Bleeding Wings Of A Love

I fell asleep in your soft foliage
in my dream you drank my spirit dry
I awoke to hear your bark swelling

for us I foresaw an endless garden
you mowed down the flowers with your eyelashes
leaving me with nothing but arid roots

together we'd raised a sea, I thought
you gathered the water in your skirts and dragged it away
I was drenched in the froth, white no more

on moonless nights I scanned your eyes for a star
with poignant words you probed my softest spots
I raked up my heart's shards with my naivety

and here I am, on the bleeding wings of a love
you wrote me off long ago, after all
I've turned the page on you, once and for all

and opened up to poetry

Translated to English by Jonathan Ross & Numan Kılıç

بال خونین عشق

در سبزِ برگِ باغ آغوشت آرمیدم
در رویایی
جان تشنه ام را نوشیدی
از خواب بیدار شدم
تا آوای زندگی را
زیر پوست تو دریابم

آنگاه یک باغ زیبای بی انتها نمایان شد
با مژه هایت گل های باغ را درو کردی
و چیزی جز ریشه های خشک
برایم نگذاشتی

فکر می کردم
که ما دریایی را
از سر راه برداشتیم
تو آب دریا را در دامنت جمع کردی
و با خود بردی
و من با کف آبی
که دیگر سفید نبود
خیس شدم

در شب های بی مهتاب با چشمانت
در جستجوی ستاره ای بودم
با حرف های مهربانت
تمامی وجودم را پوییدی
و من با چه صداقتی
پاره پاره کردم قلب زود باورم را

اکنون این منم
بر روی بال خونین عشق

دیرگاهی است
که از یادت رفته ام
آن ورقی را که در آن می زیستی
برای همیشه برگرداندم
و پناه بردم
به دامن شعر.

Marta Markoska
Macedonia

(СТ)РАНИ НА СВЕТОТ
С(Т)РАНИ

Северот војува со Југот
Истокот со Западот
И стока да бевме
ќе видевме
во Западот се содржи
- Падот!
Во Северот е ѕверот
А Југот е некое – Друго

Во отсечки ја мериме
нашата толеранција
додека кругот му пркоси
на квадратот,
а ти ми пркосиш мене,
негодувајќи
што ќе јадеме денес!

End of the World

The Nord is in war with the South
The East with the West
Even if we were a herd
we would have understood
the West contains
-Unrest!
The North holds the Forth
And the South- the Drouth

Measuring our tolerance
in segments
while the circle defies
the square,
and you defy me,
nagging
what should we eat today!

پایان دنیا

شمال در جنگ با جنوب
و شرق با غرب

حتی اگر گله ای از حیوانات بودیم
می فهمیدیم که غرب
- ناآرامی به ارمغان می آورد
شمال در حال پیشروی است
و جنوب - در خشکسالی

سنجش آستانه تحملِ ما
چون دایره
در نفی مربع
و من و تو در نزاع
درد ما اما
دغدغه ی تکه نانی است
برای امروز.

КВАНТНА ТЕОРЕМА НА ЉУБОВТА

Ние сме како ѕвезди
што колабирале
во сопствената гравитација
и сега бестелесни
вратени во состојба нулта
го броиме времето наназад
за да тврдиме дека сè од нас почнало
и со нас завршува!

Quantum Theory of love

We are just like stars
that collapsed
in their own gravity
and now weightless
back to the zero state
we count time backwards
so, we can claim that it all started with us
and with us it shall end!

تئوری کوانتُم عشق

ما چون ستارگانی هستیم
که فرومی ریزند
و در حالت معلق
به مکان صفر بازمی گردند

اگر زمان را معکوس بشماریم
می توان گفت همه چیز
با ما شروع می شود
و با ما به پایان می رسد.

Maria Lucilia F. Meleiro
Portugal

SOLTAR A PALAVRA

Nos olhos as palavras
Nos labios o frio
No bolso os cinco tesouros de Midas
E' preciso desenhar circulos de fogo
Sobre as madrugadas glaciais
Incendiar pracas e ruas da cidade
A gritar aos quatro ventos
Que e' tempo de a palavra voltar aos labios
Cansados do pesado silencio

To unleash the words

Words in the eyes
coldness on the lips
the five treasures of Midas in the pocket
circles of fire must be drawn
on the icy frozen mornings
fire must be set on the city streets and squares
shouting from the roof top
telling to the four winds
that it is high time for the words
to come back to the lips
so tired of the heavy silence.

برای رهایی کلمات

چشم ها گویا
سردیِ لب ها
پنج گنجِ میداس[14]
پنهان

باید حلقه های آتش برپا کرد
برای صبح های یخ زده
باید در خیابان ها و میادینِ شهر
آتشی برپا شود
باید با بانگی رسا از روی بام ها
از چهارسوی سخن گفت
چرا که زمان آن فرارسیده
کلمات را بر زبان آوریم
خسته از این سکوت سنگین.

---

[14] میداس Midas، شخصیت اسطوره ای یونان باستان، سمبل حماقت و خساست.

OS INFINITOS NOS

No comeco dos nos esta o fim
E no seu fim o comeco
A meio de uma noite de verao posso ouvir musica
E encontrar palavras que nunca pensei dizer
E ver ruas que nunca pensei percorrer
Sempre a sentir o chamamento do mar numa praia distante
A ver a raiva humana de sorriso lacerado
Tardiamente revelado na consciencia das coisas
O mal feito para agravo do outro tomado como verdade
Ha que mergulhar nas aguas genesiacas
Movimentando-me com estilo
Como se dancasse
Acenando sempre
Pois comido esta o fruto da epoca passada
E as palavras do novo caminho aguardam a sua vez
Estou aqui ali e algures
O meu comeco
E nao ha fim a vista nestes nos

The endless knots

We are at the beginning of the end
and the end is the beginning
in a summer night I can hear to music
and find the words I never thought of saying
and see the streets I never wanted to walk along
always feeling inside some kind of sea calling in a distant shore
watching the human rage in a wounded smile
late revealed by the conscience of things
evil being done and taken as bare truth
one must plunge into the genesiac waters
and move in a staylish way
always waving
because the fruit of past has already been eaten
and the words of the new way wait for their turn
I am here there somewhere
my beginning
and there is no end for these knots.

گره های بی پایان

ما در آغاز پایانی هستیم
که خود آغازی است

در یک شب تابستانی
نوای آهنگی به گوشم می رسد
واژه هایی را می یابم
که هرگز نمی توانستم بیان کنم

از ساحلی دوردست
دریایی را در وجودم حس می کنم
که نغمه ای سرمی دهد

تماشای خشم انسان در لبخندِ تلخ او
و وجدانِ انسانی که
دیرهنگام بیدار می شود

شرارت و دروغ بجای حقیقت
برای شُستنِ خود از آلودگی
باید در آب زمزم غوطه خورد
چرا که فرصت های گذشته
از دست رفته اند
و واژه های نوین
در انتظار رسیدن نوبت خود هستند

من در اینجا و هر کجا
این آغاز من است
و پایان این گره ها
ناپیدا.

Isabel Miguel
Spain

En qué la lágrima

En qué la lágrima.
Si hay un talud de escombros y una mano.
Si hay una marcha-huida en el camino
y el peso del adiós rompe en la espalda.

En qué la lágrima.
Si hay hambre que es angustia y es futuro.
Si hay un temblor que llora en cada niño
y la muerte se esconde en sus zapatos.

Cuándo, dónde la lágrima.
Si una profunda arruga está tallando
su rictus de dolor en cada rostro.

El mar es tumba y llanto
para sus ojos secos.

Where the tear

Where the tear.
If there's a slope of rubble and a hand.
If there's a departure-flight on the road
 and the load of farewells breaks on one's back.

Where the tear.
If there's hunger that it's angst and future.
If there's a tremor that weeps in every child
and death hides in shoes.

When, where the tear.
If a profound line is carving
its expression of pain on each face.

The sea is graveyard and crying
for tearless eyes.

کجاست اشکی

کجاست اشکی
آنگاه که در شیب یک جاده سنگی
دستی نمایان می شود
و سنگینی وداع، کمری را
هنگام عبور از خیابان می شکند

آنجا که اشک
از ترس آینده و گرسنگی
لرزش گریه کودکی ست
و کفش های انبوهی
که گواه کشته شدگانند.

کجا و کی اشکی
آنگاه که خطوط عمیق چهره
نشانه رنج و درد است

برای چشمان بی اشک
دریا گورستانی ست
که می گرید.

NO ME SIENTO CULPABLE

Caía el sol.
La mar era un prodigio de reflejos,
acuarela que nadie pintaría
con velas blancas.

Se hizo la tarde sereno latido
de una mano en la mía
entre la fresca caricia del aire,
mirada suspendida en la cadencia
de luces enlazadas.

Y me atrapó
el colorido trémolo
de un mar-cielo de amianto.

Espumé entre las olas batientes de la orilla
hasta sentirme roca, arena y sal,
aleteé viento, me crecí en árbol,
hechizada gaviota en propio vuelo.

Fui latido en el pulso de otras venas,
y aire de tu mismo aliento...

                              ... y paz.

No me siento culpable de ser Dios
entre la eternidad de dos instantes.

I Do Not Feel Guilty

The sun was setting.
The sea was a marvel of reflections,
a watercolour that nobody would paint
with white sails.
The afternoon became a serene pulse
as a hand in mine
in the fresh caress of the air,
a look suspended in the cadence
of laced lights.

The coloured tremolo
of an asbestos sea-sky
captured me.

I foamed amongst waves beating on the shore
until I felt myself as rock, sand and salt,
I winged as wind, I grew as tree,
a seagull bewitched in full flight.

I beat as a pulse in other veins
and the air of your breath....
... and peace.

I do not feel guilty being God
between the eternity of a split second.

احساس گناه نمی کنم

غروبِ نابهنگام خورشید
اعجازِ بازتاب آن در دریا
با قایقی که بادبانِ سپیدش
دیگر قابل تصویر نیست

روز
به نبض شادی تبدیل شده
مانند دستی در دست من
در نوازش نسیمی
با نگاهی به نوسانِ ریسمانی از نور
شیفته لرزش ابر پنبه ای رنگ آسمان
روی دریا

بین امواجی که
به ساحل می کوبند
تحلیل می روم
تا آنجایی که احساس می کنم
خود سنگ و شن و نمک شده ام
مانند باد پرواز کرده
و مثل درختی قد کشیده ام

چون یک مرغ دریایی
عاشق پرواز به اوج
تپیده مثل نبضی
در رگِ دیگران
و هوای نفس تو ...
و آرامش

در میان ابدیت
و مقطع کوتاه زندگی
احساس گناه نمی کنم
که خدا شده ام.

Anna Montojo
Spain

AGUA

> *...y dame un poco de sed*
> *que me estoy muriendo de agua.*
>
> *(Carmen París. Savia nueva.)*

No sé dónde volcar el agua que rebosa
del cántaro que traigo entre mis brazos
tratando de que no se me derrame;
no quiero que se pierda sin provecho
ni que caiga en un suelo pedregoso
donde la seque el sol sin miramientos.

Quiero que al menos deje alguna huella
algún surco en la tierra
donde pueda prender algún recuerdo,
una sombra de dicha momentánea;
que acaso dé cobijo a una flor imposible
o a unas migas de pan para los pájaros.

WATER

> *...and give me some thirst*
> *for I am dying of water.*
> *(Carmen Paris, Savia Nueva)*

I don't know where to pour the water
that overflows this pitcher I am carrying,
trying not to spill over.
I don't want it to get lost with no profit,
neither to pour it on rocky ground
where it will dry hopelessly.

I want it to make some prints at least,
a groove on the ground
where some memories can seed,
a shadow of instant joy
that may give shelter
to an impossible flower,
or to some breadcrumbs for the birds.

"و کمی آب به من بدهید تا از تشنگی نمیرم"
Carmen paris, Sovia Nueva

آب

نمی دانم کجا بریزم
آب این کوزه سرریز را
که بر دوش دارم
تا نچکد روی زمین
و بیهوده هدر رود
یا بر زمین سخت بریزد
و خشک شود

می خواهم اگر آبش ریخت
لااقل نشانی از آن بجای ماند
چون شیاری روی زمین
برای شکفته شدن خاطره ها
سایه ای برای شادی این لحظه
پناهگاهی
برای یک گل نشکفته.

INVIERNO

Hace frío, de pronto ha llegado el invierno
y estoy en cueros vivos.
Sin un maldito harapo que cubra mi memoria
ni me abrigue el futuro, solo queda

este miedo agarrado a la garganta
y este odio feroz a los espejos
y este atronador silencio de los pájaros
y esta cama sembrada de espejismos

este insomnio plagado de preguntas
este frío que quema entre las piernas
esta contradicción del propio cuerpo
esta verdad forjada en mil mentiras

este gusto salobre de las lágrimas
este amargo dulzor de la derrota
esta nostalgia de lo que no existe
esta caricatura de mí misma.

Esta tristeza de vivir la muerte
y este hastío de morir la vida.
Este temblor de ausencias y recuerdos
y esta espalda vacía de tus manos.

Ha llegado el invierno, así, de pronto
y me ha encontrado sola, en cueros vivos.

Winter

It is cold, and suddenly the winter has come and I am naked.
Without a damn rag to cover my memory,
or to keep the future warm, there is only.

This fear clawing my throat,
and this fierce hatred of mirrors,
and this thunderous silence of birds,
and this bed seeded of mirages.

This insomnia crowded with questions
this cold burning between the legs
this contradiction of my own body
this true forged in a thousand lies.

This salty taste of tears
this bittersweet of defeat
this longing of what doesn't exist
this caricature of myself.

This sadness of living the death,
and this weariness of dying the life,
this tremor of absences and memories,
and my back empty of your hands.

Winter has come, suddenly,
and has found me alone, in the raw.

زمستان

هوا سرد است
و زمستان زودرس
و من برهنه
با مغزی تهی
از هر خاطره ای
برای گرم نگاه داشتن آینده
با ترسی گره خورده
در گلو
با نفرت تلخ از آینه
سکوت بی انتهای پرندگان
و سرابی از بستر اجبار

خواب از سر پریده
با یک دنیا پرسش
با سرمای سوزنده
در پاهایم
و کشمکش های درونیم

حقیقتی
با هزار دروغ ساختگی
با طعم شور اشک
و طعم تلخ شکست
و اشتیاق به آرزوهای واهی
با تصویر مسخره ای
از خود
و اندوه تجربه زندگی
با مرگ

و خسته
از مرده بودنِ زندگی
با تلنگری به خاطرات گمشده
و فقدان تو در تنهایی

هوا سرد است
و زمستانِ زودرس
مرا در بیابانی برهوت یافته.

Julio Pavanetti
Uruguay/Spain

EN UN VERSO

He querido escribir mis pensamientos,
plantear las preguntas que me inquietan,
denunciar atropellos e injusticias,
mostrar mi rebeldía ante el exceso,
mi rechazo absoluto al despotismo,
mi indignación tenaz frente al corrupto.
He querido expresar mis discrepancias,
filosofar, buscar luz en las sombras,
enfrentar las transiciones del cuerpo,
encontrarle respuestas a mis dudas.
He querido dejar sólo en un verso
-sabiendo que soy polvo y todo sobra-
un mensaje de amor para el futuro
antes de acomodarme en mi penumbra.
He querido, aguzando mi conciencia,
calcular la distancia entre la vida
y la muerte que cabe en un poeta,
pero hoy me mutilan el desánimo
y la vergüenza. Apenas tibia el sol
por detrás del cadalso de la tarde.
La aflicción es un charco que la sombra
agranda y que entorpece mi propósito
de búsqueda obstinada de un poema
que testimonie el último deseo.

In A Verse

I've wanted to write my thoughts,
raising the questions that disturb me,
denouncing outrages and injustices,
showing my rebellion opposite to the excess,
my absolute rejection of despotism,
my tenacious indignation against the corrupt.

I've wanted to express my discrepancies,
philosophizing, seeking light in the shadows,
facing the transitions of the body,
finding answers to my doubts.

I've wanted to leave only one verse
–knowing that I am only dust–
a message of love for the future
before settling into my gloom.

I've wanted, sharpening my conscience,
to calculate the distance between life and death
that fits into a poet,
but today I am mutilated
by discouragement and shame.
Just warm the sun behind the afternoon scaffold.

Affliction is a puddle that shadow enlarges
and hinders my purpose
of stubborn search of the poem
witness of my last will.

در یک شعر

خواستم که در یک شعر
افکارم و همه چیزهایی
که مرا می آزارند
به روی کاغذ بیاورم
تا کشمکش درون خود را
با خشم و عصیان
در رد استبداد و دیکتاتور بیان کنم
با افکار فیلسوفانه
در جستجوی نور
در تاریکی باشم
در حالیکه با تمام وجودم
از خود گذشته
و در عرفان سیر می کنم
خواهان پاسخی
برای سئوال ها و ابهامات هستم

خواستم که فقط در یک شعر
- آگاه به این که من چیزی جز خاک نیستم -
پیام عشق خود را
برای آیندگان بیان کنم
خواستم
مانند یک شاعر مسئول
برای وجدان بیدار خود
فاصله میان مرگ و زندگی
را بَردارم
ولی امروز
با شرمندگی و ناامیدی دریافتم
که زبان نوشتن ندارم
زبانم لال شده است
چرا که آفتاب
تنها پشت جوخه اعدام را
گرم می کند
و درد و رنج، گودال بزرگی است
که سایه ها را بزرگ تر نشان می دهد
و این خود مانع بزرگی است

که نتوانم
خواستِ درونی ام را
در شعری بیان کنم
اما این گواهِ آخرین
آرزوی من است.

NOCTURNA

Viene en nombre de todas las mujeres
a la hora en que se encienden los letreros
y envejecen los lirios de la luz.

Con el garbo sensual que luce el cisne,
llega siempre puntual como el latido
cuando el día declina y se desangra,
despejando las calles para el hombre
noctívago, bohemio y solitario.

Cubierta por un velo luminoso
que salpica su piel de transparencias,
la mujer del poema me seduce
con su andar voluptuoso, su mirada
llameante y sus labios encarnados.

Debajo de ese tul, la desnudez
de un cuerpo hecho de sueño y de rocío,
viene a darme cobijo y a librarme
de la atmósfera oscura y silenciosa
que envuelve muchas veces a mi estro.

Parece que la noche nunca acaba
pero al final los versos siempre afloran
en cópula salvaje con mi musa.

Nightly

She comes on behalf of all women
at the time the neon lights come on
and the lilies of light get old.

With the sensual panache
that the swan has
she always arrives on time as the beat
when the day declines and bleeds,
clearing the streets for the nocturnal,
bohemian, and lonely man.

Covered by a luminous veil
that splashes her skin of transparencies,
the woman of the poem seduces me
with her voluptuous walk,
her flaming gaze and her incarnate lips.

Under that tulle,
the nakedness of a body
made of sleep and dew,
comes to give me shelter
and save me of the dark
and silent atmosphere
that wraps my estrus many times.

It seems the night never ends
but finally, the verses always surface
wildly mating with my muse.

شب ها

با روشن شدن چراغ های نئون
و خاموشی آهسته نیلوفرهای نور
دیدار شبانه ام با الهه ای ست
که خرامان
هر شب می آید
با دلبری یک قو

آنگاه که روز مشقت بار
به سر می رسد
و خیابان ها تهی می شوند
از مردان تنها
و دیگر پرسه زنندگان شب

با هاله ای از نور
می فریبد مرا در یک شعر
با گام های دلبرانه
و نگاه آتشین
و لب شکرخایش
در زیر آن لباس نور
بر روی پوست برهنه اش
که از خواب و شبنم ساخته شده
می آید برای نجات من
از این سیاهی بی پایان
که در برگرفته همه وجود مرا

آنگاه
شعر در من جاری می شود
با شور و عشق
می آمیزد
و یگانه می شود
با الهه زیبایی.

Ljubica Perkman
Bosnia- Herzegovina/ Germany

Voljela bih

Voljela bih da sam pauk,
da razapnem zlatnu mrežu,
da se ljudi tu prepletu,
da se zbliže i povežu.
Iako je nevidljiva
razapeta mreža meka,
tanke niti isplela bih
od čovjeka do čovjeka.
Voljela bih da sam pauk,
i da pletem, pletem sada,
npreglednu, čvrstu mrežu,
do svakoga sela, grada.
Voljela bih da sam pauk,
da opletem mrežu svijeta,
uplela bih samo Ljubav,
kad se javi, kad procvjeta.

Ich wünschte mir

Ich wünschte mir,
ich wäre eine Spinne.
Ich würde ein goldenes
Spinnennetz weben,
damit sich Menschen
darin verfangen,
sich näherkommen
und zu einander gelangen.
Auch wenn das Netz
unsichtbar und noch
so dünn ist,
ich würde es spinnen
von Mensch zu Mensch.
Ich wünschte,
ich wäre eine Spinne,
dann würde ich weben
und weben,
ein festes Netz zu jedem Dorf
und jeder Stadt.
Ich wünschte,
ich wäre eine Spinne,
ich würde die ganze
Welt einweben,
nur Liebe soll enthalten sein,
wenn sie sich meldet und erblüht...

ای کاش

ای کاش عنکبوتی بودم
و با تارهای طلایی خود
توری می بافتم
تا در انسجام آن
انسان ها در کنار یکدیگر
دوستی را دریابند
گرچه این تور ناپیداست
می بافتم آن را

ای کاش عنکبوتی بودم
که با تارهای طلایی خود
شهرها، دهکده ها
و همه دنیا را
به یکدیگر می تابیدم
تا در انسجام آن
عشق شکوفا شود.

Nikad nije kasno

Nikad nije kasno
izreći
lijepu riječ,
riječ što se
u nama pritajila,
kao ljubav.

Nikad nije kasno
pokloniti cvijet
koji je dugo čekao
u tami daleke šume.

Es ist niemals zu spät

Es ist niemals zu spät,
ein nettes Wort auszusprechen,
ein Wort, das sich in uns verborgen,
wie die Liebe.

Es ist niemals zu spät,
eine Blume zu schenken,
die lange gewartet hat
im Dunkel eines fernen Waldes.

هرگز دیر نیست

هرگز دیر نیست
برای کلامی محبت آمیز
کلامی که در سینه ما پنهان است
واژه عشق

هرگز دیر نیست
گلی را پیشکش کنیم
که در دوردست جنگلی انبوه
منتظر چیده شدن است.

Khader Salfij
Syrian

الجيوش

جنود أنهكهم المشي خلف النجوم على أكتاف قادتهم الحجريين.
يمضغون الصمت والثوم.
ينامون في العراء.
لا يقتلون.
بل يُقتلون.
هم النجوم الحزينة، مثلي.

Armies

Soldiers tired of walking behind
the stars on the shoulders
of their stony commanders.
They chew silence and garlic.
They sleep in the open air.
They don't kill.
Rather, they are killed.
They are sad stars, like me.

سربازان

سربازان، خسته از گام برداشتن
به دنبال فرماندهان جنایتکار
با ستاره هایی روی شانه هایشان
در سکوت
توتون و تنباکو می جوند
و زیر آسمان
دور از خانه می خوابند

آنها نمی کُشند
زیرا خود دیری است
که گُشته شده اند
آنها ستارگان غمگینی هستند
مانند من.

موت البحيرة

كيف لي أن أقنع البجع بموت البحيرة، وأنا أرى الزرقة تودّعُ عيناهُ، الآن، فيما جناحاه ترتبكان بصمتٍ
كيف لي أن أقنعَ مُقل العابرين ، وأنا أرى بياض رقصه الذي ما عاد يعتليه؟
كان عليّ أن أقنع نفسي بجلالة حزنه
كي لا ننتهي جميعا إلى فزع غامض
ولم نجد الوقت كي نقنع العابرين
هناك،
في المنفى،
بموت البحيرة.

Lake death

How can I convince the swan of the lake's death,
when I see the blue bidding its eyes,
now, while its wings are silently swaying.
How can I convince the passersby,
when I see the whiteness of his dance, which no longer tops it?
I had to convince myself of the majesty of his grief
lest we all end up in a mysterious panic.
We did not find time to convince the passersby
there,
in exile,
Lake death.

مرگ دریا

چگونه می توانم خبر مرگ دریا را
به قو بدهم
آنگاه که عشق به دریا
و بازتاب رنگ آبی آن را
در چشمان او می بینم
آنگاه که بال هایش به آرامی
هوای پرواز به آن سوی دارند

چگونه می توانم به این رهگذر بگویم
که دیگر رقص زیبایش
در دریای مرده و بی روح
شکوه خود را از دست داده است

گویی می بایست
عظمت اوج اندوهش را باور کنم
تا در پایان این دردِ مشترک نابود نشویم
زیرا ما فرصتی برای گفتگو نداشتیم

آنجا، در تبعیدگاه،
مرگ دریا.

Agron Shele
Albania

Pasazh

Më duhet të shikoj përtej kornizave
e kontrastin ta kthej në një ngjyrë më shumë
për të deshifruar të gjitha pamjet
që brenda një çasti ndryshojnë kaq shumë,
ta bëjnë atë det e tajfun
por dhe paqe që fle mbi të bardhën valë
tek prehet ndanë një ishulli
që për mua mbetet përherë Itakë.

Kohë që fle mbi zambakë të çelur
qerthullit ndritur në pranverë
tek mbledh rrezet e para të agimit
e fsheh vështrimin përtej perëndimit,
si mbledh më pas kumtrin yje
e feks në kopshtin e dashuruar të qershive
për të ndjerë fëshfërimën e largët trupit
që poshtë shallit të mallit mbështillet.

E dita nis me tjetër tis
tek vrapon dlirësisë jetë
heq një fashë që përtheyen dritën
e kthehet në sharm që përshfaqet me diellin,
endur ashtu në zjarrin e zotave
e lirës që vjen muzës perëndi
gjurmëve mbetur në deshira fjalësh
a mallit të etur mbi gjurmë buzësh.

Passage

I need to see beyond the frames
and twist the contrast to make one more colour
for deciphering all the views
that in a second change so abruptly
to make that colour a sea, a typhoon,
but also, the peace that sleeps on the white waves
peace that rests beside an island
which, for me, Ithaca always remains

Time sleeps on the blooming lilies
collecting the first beams of dawn
and hiding their sight beyond the twilight
putting together the galaxy of stars.
that sparks on the cherry garden of love
to feel the distant whisper of the body
wrapped in a scarf of longing

And so, the day's vail is unveiled
running toward the purity of life
removing a fraction that reflects the light
and turning it to a charm that reveals the sun
weaved like this, in Gods fire
together with the lyre of the goddess of muses
at the footsteps left on the desire of words
or the thirsty longing for the traces of lips.

گذرگاه

باید فراسوی چارچوب ها
را ببینم
آنگاه با چرخش رنگ های متضاد
می توان رنگ دیگری آفرید
برای درک منظری دیگر
که در آنی دگرگون می شود
تا این رنگ بدل شود
به دریا و طوفانی

سکوتی که روی امواج سپید دریا
می نشیند
یادآور آرامش حاکم بر
جزیره ی ایتاکا[15] ست

زمان در میان شکوفه های نیلوفر
در انتظار طلوع سپیده دم می ایستد
و در پشت گرگ و میش سحرگاه
پنهان می شود

آنگاه همه ستارگانِ کهکشان
یکی شده
با درخشش عشق در باغِ آلبالو
برای شنیدن زمزمه ای در دوردست
سرشار از اشتیاقی پنهانی اند
و روز، آمیخته با جانِ پاکِ زندگی
آغاز می شود
و حرکت ذره ای از نور
اعجازِ تابش خورشید
چونان آتشی ست
هم کیش خدایان
همراه با لِییِر[16]، الهه موسیقی و هنر
در آرزوی واژه های گمشده
و آغوش و بوسه ای.

---

[15] ایتاکا Ithaka، نام جزیره ای در ساحل غربی یونان.
[16] لِییِر Lyre، الهه ی موسیقی و هنر در اساطیر یونان.

Sa larg dhe sa afër

Sa larg dhe sa afër,
me gjymtyrë të mbetura kohëve trishtim,
endur shtjellave gri të pakumtimësië
tek e përshpirtshmja mllef dhe angullimë.

Sa larg dhe sa afër,
ne poseduesit e lirisë angshtim
kufijve dhe horizonteve të humbura
udhëkryqeve të fateve trazim.

Sa larg dhe sa afër,
magjisë rishfaqur vegim
te etshëm pas krenarisë boshe
dhe rrugëve tona pa kthim.

Sa larg dhe sa afër,
prekjes së ëndrrës më të bardhë
tek e nesërmja shpresë dhe nganjëdhim
tek e dlirta, thjeshtësi në madhështi .

How far away and nearby

How fare and how close,
With knees that remain through the times of sadness,
Spreading through grey waves of confusion
To genuine soul, anger and sadness.

How far and hour close,
We the owners of freedom and angst
In the bridges and lost horizons
In the intersections of turbulent fates.

How far and how close,
In the magic that has appeared at dawn
With thirst after an empty pride
And through the streets without a return.

How far and how close,
Touching the whitest dreams
At tomorrow's hope and frightens
At the simplest humility, greatness.

Translated into English by Merita Paparisto

چه غریب، چه آشنا

چه غریب، چه آشنا
با زانوانی که در دورانِ غم و اندوه
برجای می خشکند
با سردرگمی
در میان امواج خاکستری
با جانی منزه اما خشمگین

چه غریب، چه آشنا
ما صاحبان بیم و آزادی
از پل ها و افق های گم شده
در تقاطع سرنوشت های آشفته

چه غریب، چه آشنا
شیفته ی طلوع سپیده دم
تشنه ی غروری بی محتوا
از خیابان های بی بازگشت

چه غریب، چه آشنا
لمس رویاهای بی آلایش
بیم و امید از فردا
به سادگی یک فروتنی
با بزرگواری.

Andy Siege
Kenya/ Germany/ Iran

Mirror

When the mirror finally breaks
there will be beauty in the shards
when the sky's athunder and lightning
lightning sets the tree on fire

And when the pixelated souls
disappear into the sky
will be when hordes of angel's fly
oh lunatic moon
I'm howling at you
please tell me more about your gloom
oh wild sun
so high at noon
you make the roses in my garden bloom

The devil drowned me in the river
he didn't know that I have gills
the devil chucked me in the fire
luckily, I was born with scales

آینه

در تکه خُرده های آینه شکسته
زیبایی نمایان است هنوز
و آذرخش در پی رعد و برق
به آتش می کشد
درخت را

و جان های سرگردانی
که در آسمان محو می شوند
گویی فرشتگانی اند
که پرواز می کنند

آه ای ماه سرگشته
از اندوه خود برایم بگو
و تو ای خورشید زیبا
که نیمروز در اوج آسمان
رُزهای باغم را
به شکوفه می نشانی

آنگاه که اهرمن
مرا در آب غرق کرد
نمی دانست
که آبشش دارم
و وقتی مرا به آتش کشاند
نمی دانست
دگربار با فلس زاده می شوم.

LUNATIC MOON

Oh, lunatic moon
your wise white wink
your gloom
curse thee and thy splendorous glitter
curse thee and thy generous shine
and look upon this world so bitter
and taste these crimson tears of mine

ماه سرگشته

آه ای ماه سرگشته
ای فرزانه
با اینکه اندوهگینی
با گوشه چشم
کرشمه می کنی
نفرین بر تو و
فروغ درخشانت
نفرین بر تو و
بخشش نور تابانت
بنگر درد و رنج این دنیا را
تا حس کنی طعم اشک های
خونینم را.

Annabel Villar
Uruguay/Spain

EN TRÁNSITO

> *La vida es más ancha que larga*
> Gregorio MARAÑÓN

E inesperadamente,
atravesamos el umbral.

En la otra orilla hallamos
el silencio y relojes alterados,
se calman los vientos y la borrasca,
se acallan las furias y el sonido.

Otra vez desnudos y desarmados,
ya sin bagajes ni recetas,
cruzamos a solas porque Caronte
no está allí para guiarnos.

Por fin desaparecen
las expectativas y
los prolegómenos,
y la paz llega.

IN TRANSIT

Out of the blue
we are crossing the threshold
and finding the silence
and the altered watches
on the opposite side.

Winds and storms get soothe,
furies and sound get silenced.

Naked and unarmed again
and without baggage or directions,
we cross alone because
Charon is not there to guide us.

Finally,
expectations and prelims vanish
and peace comes.

در آستانه

سراسیمه از آستانه عبور می کنیم
در آن سوی، خاموشی
و ساعت هایی با حرکت معکوس عقربه ها

باد و طوفان به سکون رسیده
خشم و هیاهو به خاموشی

عریان و بی ساز و برگ
بدون بار و جامه ای
یا راهنمایی
به تنهایی از آستانه عبور می کنیم
هنوز دربان به انتظار ما نِشَسته

در پایان
چشمداشت ها و پیشداوری ها
محو شده
و آرامش ابدی هویدا میگردد.

ALICIA DETRÁS DEL ESPEJO

> *"Alicia: ¿Cuánto tiempo es para siempre?*
> *Conejo Blanco: A veces sólo un segundo"*
> Lewis CARROLL

Alicia no sabía que detrás del espejo
no existía un país de maravillas.
Ni tampoco sabía -mientras se deslizaba-

que no había luz al final del túnel.

Sólo estaba la vida cotidiana
secuestrando las horas privada de la sangre
que corre por las venas y la acerca a la muerte,

metástasis de vida.

Sin embargo la tentaba el olvido
colándose en el frasco de la calma,
la muerte como pausa, la vida como tránsito,
sin golpes, sin ofensas,
sólo con la reina de corazones
que detenía el tiempo en el reloj
del conejo y su chaleco.

ALICE BEHIND THE MIRROR

Alice did not know that behind the mirror
there was no Wonderland.
Nor did she know-as she slipped-
that there was no light at the end of the tunnel.

There was only the everyday life
kidnapping the hours deprived of blood
that runs through the veins
and brings her close to death,
metastasis of life.

However, she was tempted by oblivion
sneaking into the jar of calm,
death as a pause, life as a transit,
without blows, without offenses,
only with the Queen of Hearts
who stopped the time in the watch
of the rabbit with vest.

Colored pills rolled
from the pocket of her apron,
never again would there be moments
hostages of daily life
as Alice's barge began its final journey
to the land of childhood and freedom.

آلیس در پشت آینه

آلیس نمی دانست که
در پشت آینه سرزمین عجایبی
وجود ندارد
وقتی که او در دنیای خیالی اش
سُر می خورد
نمی دانست که انتهای تونل
روشن نیست
آنچه که بود
- فقط یک زندگی عادی بود-
آنگاه که خون
در رگ هایش جاری بود
لحظه های زندگی
از دستش سُر می خوردند
و او در گذر از بحران سخت زندگی
با هر قدم
به مرگ نزدیک تر می شد

گمان فراموشی او را وسوسه کرد
و او پا به دنیای رویا گذاشت
آنجا که مرگ متوقف شده
و زندگی فقط محل عبور بود
آنجا که درد و رنج
یا آزاری وجود نداشت
آنجا که سلطان قلب ها
گذشت زمان را
به سکون درآورده بود

خرگوشی با جلیقه و پیشبندی
نشسته واز جیب هایش
آبنبات های رنگی پخش می کرد

در آنجا دیگر هیچگاه
در بَندِ زندگی روزمره نبود
آخرین سفر آلیس او را
به سرزمین آزادی کودکی اش بُرد.

Prof. Ph Dr. Mária Bátorová, DrSc. (Institute of World Literature, Slovak Academy of Sciences, German literature, Slavic literatures, comparative literature). For political reasons she was banned from publishing until 1989. After them 15 books. She is a Member of the Scientifique Society of the SAS. In 1995 - 1998 she taught at the University of Cologne in Cologne, Germany. In 2011 she founded the Center for research in comparative literature KDĎ at the Pedagogical faculty of Comenius University. In her 8 scientific monographs and other articles she studies the problematique of repressed and tabooized themes of Slovak literary history of the 20th Century. Using a new comparative method, she reconstructs the place of Slovak literary modernism in the context of European literary modernism. As a literary author and essayist, she published Since 1989 also 7 books -- novels and poems, Selection of poetry Deserts and oases (2008), novel The Center (2010), translated to German as Mitte (2018). Her works were translated into 17 languages: Monograph Jozef Cíger Hronský und die europäische Moderne (Jozef Cíger Hronský and European modernism, Veda SAV 2000), Monograph Dominik Tatarka - slovenský Don Quijote (Dominik Tatarka - The Slovak Don Quijote) published by Veda in 2012 (Dominik Tararka the slovak Don Quixote. Freedom and Dreams, vydavateľstvo Peter Lang, Wien/ Veda Bratislava 2015). She has received a number of awards including the Ľudovít Štúr Medal for outstanding scholarly contribution awarded by the President of the Slovak Academy of Sciences.

Soledad Benages Amorós, (1955, L'Alcora- España), Degree in Hispanic Philology. Master in Pedagogy and Education Sciences and Creativity. Spanish Language and Literature's professor and speaker. Specialist in Theater for Education and Curricular Adaptations for Diversity. Writes in Spanish and Catalan. Activist of the Word, she coordinates and takes part in Tertulias, Workshops, Poetry Books, Recitals and Encounters of national / international poetry. Sipea-Peru's ambassador in Spain; Member Circle of ambassadors of peace, Suisse/France; Member of the UEA Tarija-Bolivia and others movements of international poetic festivals. She has published in collective Antologies in Spain, Portugal, Germany, Cuba, Chile, Bolivia, Argentina, Perú, Dominican Republic, Paraguay, Taiwan, Mongolia, Nepal, Kurdistan, India. In-person and virtual articipation in numerous meetings and national and international poetry festivals. Poetry translated into English, Chinese, Hindi and Portuguese. Published poetry books: Soledumbre, Perú, 2016; Cronófago, Spain, 2017; Crónica del descenso al abismo, Spain, 2023.

Giovanna Benedetti, born in Panama City, Republic of Panama, Giovanna Benedetti holds a doctorate in Law and Political Science from the Autonomous University of Barcelona and the Complutense University of Madrid. A poet, short story writer and essayist, he has won the Ricardo Miró National Literature Prize in Panama six times, as well as the José Martí International

Journalism Prize in Cuba and the historical essay prize from the Simón Bolívar University in Barranquilla, Colombia.

She is a member of the Panamanian Academy of Language and was general director of the National Archives of Panama. She has worked as an expert in Copyright and Cultural Law for UNESCO and the Regional Centre for the Promotion of Books in Latin America and the Caribbean (CERLALC). She is also a ceramic sculptor, painter and graphic designer. He has lived for more than a decade in San Lorenzo de El Escorial, Madrid, Spain.

Dieter J. G. Brumm, writer, poet, journalist, born 1929 in Wentorf near Hamburg (Germany), passed away 2020 in Hamburg. Studied philosophy by Martin Heidegger in Freiburg. A freelance journalist for Norddeutscher Rundfunk (North German broadcast media) and the Süddeutsche Zeitung (South German Newspaper), he was an editorial journalist for the humanities at Spiegel magazine. He was media officer for the Industrial Union Medien and chairman of the Culture and Trillions Committee of the German Cultural Council in Bonn, as well as press spokesman for Amnesty International.

Antonio Capilla Loma, from Seville, moved to Madrid at the age of 8, where he continues to reside. With a degree in Hispanic Philology from the Complutense University of Madrid and a Diploma in Teaching, specializing in Spanish language and literature, he has been a professor of

Spanish language and literature for 37 years. Published works: Y EL CORAZÓN AL VIENTO, author's edition, Madrid, 1991; VIENTO DEL SUR, Editorial Huerga y Fierro, Madrid, 2009; EL FUEGO EN LA PALABRA, Editorial Huerga y Fierro, Madrid, 2012; EL ÁGUILA DE FUEGO CON LAS ALAS DEL TIEMPO, Editorial Huerga y Fierro, Madrid, 2013; LÚA, bilingual edition in Spanish and Galician, Editorial Lastura, Madrid, 2013; LÚA - 2nd extended edition in Spanish and Galician, Editorial Lastura, Madrid, 2016; PIEDRA DE LA HONDA, Editorial Vitruvio, Madrid, 2016;
HACIA LA LUZ, Vitruvio Publishing House, Madrid, 2020. In the process of editing EL PULSO DEL ENIGMA.His poems have also been published in numerous anthologies and literary magazines.

Metin Cengiz, Turkey; 1953 is 69 years old. He has published 17 poems, 23 essay-review-theoretical books on poetry, a total of 39 books. His poems are in translated into 32 languages in total. 18 poetry books have been published in 17 foreign countries (selected poems or translation of one of his books). He translated and published the works of 19 foreign poets into Turkish. He has prepared, translated and published two anthologies of French, one Italian and one Spanish poetry. In Turkey, files on his poetry were prepared in magazines and symposiums were organized. More than 100 critics, poets, essayists and philosophers have written on his poetry. He was interviewed in more than 200 magazines and newspapers. He participated in literature programs on radio and television and read poetry. It has taken a respectable place in all anthologies in Turkey. He participated in many festivals organized in Turkey and abroad, and spoke at symposiums. He was given a certificate of appreciation and participant in these festivals. He received the four most important poetry awards in Turkey. His writings on poetry have been translated into French, Romanian, Italian, Spanish and English and published in magazines. In France, his poems have been published in Europe and many magazines. He has six important poetry awards abroad. He has published four books of criticism about his poems.

Silvia Cuevas-Morales, was born in Chile. In 1975, she migrated to Australia and in the late 90s she settled down in Spain, where she has worked as an editor, freelance journalist and literary translator. Her work has been published in more than thirty international anthologies and has been translated into many languages. Her poetry books include: Purple Temptations (1994); Respiro de arena (1996); Al filo de la memoria/At memory's edge (2001); Canto a Némesis (2003); Rodaré maldiciendo (2008); Poliamora (2010); Desarrelament i altres poemes / Desarraigo y otros poemas (2012); and Apátrida: Diario de un Destierro/ Stateless: Diary of an Exile (2017, 2018). She has published two short story books: Nanas lésbicas: para conciliar el sueño (2013, 2016 and 2019) and El tren del miedo y otros relatos (2015 and 2019), as well as two extensive dictionaries of women in history and in literature: De la "A" a la "Z": Diccionario universal de autoras que escriben en castellano, siglo XX (2003) and Diccionario de centenarias ilustres: 100 mujeres que cambiaron la historia (2011). Among her prizes, Silvia recibed the "Grand Prix des Arts", awarded by the International Orient-Occident Academy (Romania, 2011) and "Participating we Create Spaces of Equality", prize awarded by the Women's Council of the City of Madrid (2016).

Maria do Sameiro Barroso, currently living in Lisbon (Portugal) is a medical doctor, a Germanist and a global, multilingual and awarded poet, translator, essayist, scholar and researcher in Portuguese and German Literature, Translations Studies and History of Medicine. She is a Member of Honour of the Association Alia Mundi from Serbia, and an Ambassador of Literacy and Culture of the ASIM SASAMI INDONESIA GLOBAL WRITERS of Indonesia, Intercontinental President of the Portuguese Speaking Countries of the Unión Hispanomundial de Escritores (E.H.E.) and honorable Adviser of the Poetry and Literature World Vision Facebook Group from Bangladesh, and the Portuguese translator of the "Poem of the Week", Point Editions (Belgium/Spain).

Hasan Erkek, as a poet, a playwright and a professor of drama, he has been awarded more than 20 national and international prizes. He published 26 artistic and scientific books in 14 different countries. His poetry books have been published in Turkey, France, Bulgaria, Cameroon and Romania. Some his poems have been composed by different composers from different countries. His works in his academic career have focused on the art of drama. His plays were performed by more than 40 theatres from different countries, including primarily Turkish national theatres. Furthermore, he wrote radio plays (approximately 20 radio plays were broadcast by national radios in Turkey) and film scripts (some of them were filmed). One of his specialization fields is theatre for children. Hasan Erkek took part and presented papers in many international theatre festivals and symposia. He has more than a hundred articles published in various journals and newspapers. He has been giving play reading, dramaturgy, dramatization, creative writing, drama techniques and contemporary theatre courses in various departments of universities. Hasan Erkek has worked as an Executive Board Member and Vice-president in ASSITEJ Turkey, and the president of Turkish Playwrights and Play Translators Association as well as the Head of the Department of Performing Arts at Anadolu University.

Gertrud Hauck, born in the previous century in Fischamend in Lower Austria. Acting has been her hobby for years beside her profession, but became a victim of her intensive professional commitment in strategic procurement. For plenty of years the love of performing was at last the begin of writing short stories, poems and moderation presentings of lections from comedy to tragedy. Participation in divers literary genres. Since more than 20 years an active member of the Hainburger Autorenrunde. Writing serves the amusement on one thing. Publication in divers anthologies, dramaturgy, Moderation and recitation of different programs.

Heidi Heine, born in 1955 in the Eastern part of Germany. In 1972 she passed her high school diploma for economics with a commercial qualification. Until 1978 she worked in the sales department of a state-owned company. From 1978 to 1990 she ran a private metal construction company with her husband. She founded her own assembly company in 1991 and worked worldwide until 2012. In 2012 she merged with her husband's steel construction company. From 2013 she devoted herself to working as an author and published her first novel in 2015. To date, two more novels have been published by her.

Petra M. Jansen, is a German freelance writer, instructional designer and journalistic staff. Her work also includes coaching, consulting artists / artist accompaniment and strategic marketing concepts for artists and advertising. She also works as a freelance columnist for various categories (online) in the field of social criticism, satire, ethics, journalism, music, art. Her present works find you in several German anthologies and in her own five books of poetry (Sex God Soul, [h]eis[s] kalte [W] Orte, Black Poetry, Gereimnisse &

Wahrseiten; Sinnwaisen, Satt statt stark) which are published. She stands for the opposites, from soft to hard – always at the limit of what is possible. Critical, social, emotional and startlingly, she tries to make things happen and change and stands for the freedom of thought and action with heart and mind.

Bahar Kazemi, (German/Iranian), born in 1994 in Cologne. She studied social work and pedagogy in Ludwigsburg and has been working as a pedagogue in various youth welfare institutions since 2019. She has been writing poetry since her school days. Bahar's poems are published in the anthology Frankfurt Library (Frankfurter Bibliothek) 2014 and in the anthology Library of German Language Poems (Bibliothek deutschsprachiger Gedichte) XVI 2015.

Jutta Lehmann, novelist and poet, born in Berlin in 1937. She studied religious pedagogy. She worked as a teacher at Düsseldorf secondary school religion, art and music until 1997. Publications: „Requiem for a friend" (1998), „She died in my arms" (2001), „Judith and the head of Holofernes" (2005), „Wohlvertraut" (2007), „Finding the Duwort" (2011), „Is a love" (2014), „Silhouettes" (2017) and „Shades" (2023).

Helene Levar, born in Vienna, lives in Vienna and Wolfsthal; active as a lawyer (law studies at the University of Vienna), actress (trained at the Krauss Drama School), singer, director, author, seminar leader, ... Engaged at the Vorarlberg State Theater in Bregenz and at various Viennese theaters. Founder (1992) and artistic director of the Summer Festival Wolfsthal, founder of the cultural association Ciarivari. 2001 Founder and artistic director of the cultural space „Wiener Theaterkeller". Writes mainly poems and stories. Poetry volume „Die Fledermaus sieht gar nicht mausig aus" (2017), lyrical drama „Angelica" about the life of the painter Angelika Kaufmann (2015). Publications in numerous anthologies.

Jana Machacova, In Slovakia born, Jana Machacova studied translation and interpretation of German and Russian languages at the Faculty of Arts, Comenius University in Bratislava, obtaining a master's degree. After moving to California, USA, she studied English at Los Angeles Valley College in Van Nuys, where she also attended child development classes and obtained an occupational certificate in Child Development. She worked in a preschool and later as an apartment manager in Van Nuys and Northridge. After returning to Slovakia, she supplemented her pedagogical education and worked as a teacher of English and German languages at a high school. She is one of the founders of the International Women's Club in Piestany. At high school, she successfully led two international projects Comenius which were carried out within the framework of the European Union. As part of an international project, she developed a Slovak-English dictionary of gastronomy with professional terms for waiters and cooks. She is a member of the Austrian Literary Association Hainburger Autorenrunde, where she translates texts from German into English if necessary.

Marta Markoska, was born on 29.06.1981 in Skopje, Macedonia. She holds a Bachelor of General and Comparative Literature and a Master of Cultural Studies in Literature from the Institute of Macedonian Literature in Skopje. Markoska is a member of the Writers Association of Macedonia. She has published FOURTEEN (14) books: She has written theater reviews for the Dnevnik newspaper; movie reviews, and articles on culture for several Macedonian web sites. She is a creator of two multimedia performances, and also a musical illustrator on several documentaries. Her PhD thesis is on hold to some indefinite/unspecified/uncertain time or until she figure out why the hell she has a need of it at all.

Erwin Matl., Born in 1953 in Vienna, he worked as a teacher and was involved in various foreign projects in the tourism and literature sector (including with the Czech Republic, Poland and Slovakia). The establishment of the „Hainburger Autorenrunde" (1990) made around a hundred national and international members a literary field of activity possible. The group of authors symbolically became a sign of the new beginnings in Eastern Europe in the easternmost city of Austria. In eleven youth competitions, Erwin Matl and his fellow authors created a platform for young people, which hundreds of young authors also made ample use of. There is a special network as well as artistic friendships with Hainburg's twin cities Rodgau (Germany) and Šamorín (Slovakia). - Erwin Matl mainly writes short prose, cheerful satirical poetry, meditation texts and has also published some local chronicles. Editor of 25 publications by the Hainburger Authors' Group and several spiritual books. Rediscovery and publication of the autobiographical work „Wridol's Memories" by the important Austrian exile author Boris Brainin as a German-language first publication (Pilum Literatur Verlag, 2019). In 2019, on his co-initiative, the Russian-German anthology "Humanity overcomes Borders" with 31 international authors who successfully went on a reading tour in several countries was published by Pilum Literatur Verlag.

Sylvia Meise, (meise&meise) Feelance writer and photographer based in Frankfurt/Main. Works for print and online media as well as on free projects. More under https://meiseundmeise-blog.de. Works, readings, awards KiR-Kunstpreis, Oberroden, 2022 Reise- und Reportage-Fotografie-Festival ", Schömberg, 2021 Poetry Reading with Martin Bullinger, Milchsackfabrik Frankfurt, 2018 Photography Festival „Wiesbadener Fototage "2017 Poetry Festival, Oberroden 2016.

Maria Lucilia F. Meleiro, Poet, novelist, playwriter, essayist, translator. Born in Lisbon (Portugal). Studies in English and German literature,

M.B.A. (Lisbon University). Published four historical novels- Rose of Alexandria, Irak Tears of Ishtar, The Masks of Passion, The Last Message of J.C.; two essays-German Mythology and Finisterra; two poetry books- Flower of Caos and Unpredictable Connections. Published also many poems and short stories in several national and international anthologies and literary magazines. Translator of German and American writers. Her work has been translated into English, French, Spanish, Italian, Rumanian and Arabic. In 2018-22 Maria Lucilia F. Meleiro was awarded three international literary prizes (France and Lebanon).

Isabel Miguel, Poet and translator. Her poems and translations have been published in numerous national and international magazines, as well as in more than fifty Spanish and foreign anthologies. She has published in Los libros de Umsalua the poetry collection Desvanes mínimos (Seville, 2011) and Desvanes mínimos Antología / Sobrados mínimos in Lastura Publishing House (2013). She has translated the poems of the Indian poet Bina Sarkar in the poetry collection Cercana Lejanía, as well as multiple authors in single poems. Her poems have been translated into French, English, Bulgarian, Italian, Romanian, Galician, Catalan, Portuguese and Arabic. She has taken part in numerous national and international poetry meetings, having directed the 1st International Meeting of the United Nations of Letters in Ronda (Malaga). She is a member of the editorial board of Editorial Lastura, where she directs the poetry collections Alcalima and Diezynueve. member of the board of directors of the feminist association of women poets Genial ogías.

Ana Montojo, was born in Madrid (Spain). In 1998 her poem When you come back won the „Carmen Conde" poetry prize from the Majadahonda City Council, and in 2010 her first collection of poems, The mist of time, was awarded the „Blas de Otero" prize from the same institution. In 2012 she published her second collection of poems, Indoor plants, in the publishing house "Cuadernos del Laberinto". In 2015 the third, Living with the bare minimum, edited by Huerga y Fierro. In 2016 This thunderous silence of the birds and JAIME, in Lastura editions; in 2017 Borrowed time, in ACCI editions and in 2018 she won the "Nicolás del Hierro" poetry prize with her collection of poems A sax solo. In 2019 she published Collateral damages, with Huerga y Fierro and won the "José Gerardo Manrique de Lara" prize with her poem Too late. In 2021 she published her anthology As if this were not enough, also with Huerga y Fierro. In the field of narrative, she has published two novels: Secret memories of a wellborn girl (2014) and Losers (2022), both in the publishing house ATLANTIS. She has participated in different anthologies, such as Umpteenth page; Love, contemporary love poetry (Cuadernos del Laberinto); Erotizhadas (Unaria Ediciones), Love is written without blood (Lastura), against sexist violence, We shelter, in favor of the NGO ProActiva Open Arms, Against, poetry against repression, and Salam bilingual anthology of Spanish-Arabic poetry. She has collaborated in various literary magazines (Álora, The blank blue sheet, Millstone).

Julio Pavanetti, (Montevideo, Uruguay, 1954), He is a poet living in Benidorm, Spain. President of the international poet's association "Liceo Poético de Benidorm". Associate Academic and Honorary Member of the North American Academy of Modern Literature. Director of the poetry collection „Azul" of Enkuadres Publishers, Spain. Director of the Benidorm International Poetry Festival (FIPBECO). Member of the Association of Spanish Writers and Artists. Member of the Spanish Collegiate Association of Writers. Titular member of the Tomitana Academy (Romania). He has published twelve poetry books, one of them, "The spiral of time" in Romanian/Spanish bilingual edition, published in Bucarest, Romania in 2012. His book "At the touch of a silent flesh", won the first prize in the contest of Aspe, Spain, in 2015, and was published in 2018 in English/Spanish bilingual edition. His book "Mërgimi Dhemb" (Exile hurts) was published in 2021 in Albania and Kosovo in Albanian language. His book "Battute d'arresto" was published in Italy in Italian language in 2022. He had received many awards and recognitions, both for his poetry as for his cultural work. In 2021 he received the Award of Excellence for his Career in Rome, Italy, and won the 1st prize for foreign poets of the VIII Edition of the „Città del Galateo - Antonio De Ferraris" International Excellence Award, Rome, Italy. He has participated in several poetry festivals and took part in more than 100 international anthologies. Many of his poems have been translated into 27 languages and have been published on innumerable Spanish and international literary magazines.

Ljubica Perkman, Poet, novelist, Author for children's books and illustrator. Born 1948 in Celinac near Banja Luka in today´s Bosnia and Herzegovina. She graduated from the medical college in Banja Luka as pharmaceutical technician. Since 1969 she lives in Germany. As a commercial employee, she worked for an American IT company for over twenty-six years. She devoted her free time to poetry and summed up her love and affinity to the distant homeland in poems and verses. Numerous publications followed in various community works, newspapers, blogs and magazines worldwide. The first own bilingual book was published in 1996 and then followed by nine more of poems, short stories and collage novels. She received a diploma for successful participation in the cycle of fine arts in 2015 at the „Summer Art Workshop" in Crikvenica, Croatia. In 2012, a painting by her was issued on the occasion of the 200th anniversary of the Grimm Brothers as a special stamp in Vienna. She was active in numerous clubs and associations, as well as amateur theater actress. She is a member of the „Writers Association SIEBEN e.V." Frankfurt, Art Association KiR in Rödermark and honorary member of the Hainburg Authors' Circle in Austria and the association of "Liceo Poetico de Benidorm". www.ljubicaperkman.de

Boris Pfeiffer, was born in Berlin in 1964. After graduating from high school, he became a bookseller and cab driver, studied linguistics and later screenwriting at the Berlin Film Academy, dffb. He worked as an assistant director and director at theaters in Germany and Switzerland. In 1994 his first play for children was performed. In 2003 his first children's book was published. Since then, he has written many children's books, plays and musicals. His latest works: „Survivors" and „Earth. Water.Fire. Storm. To Survive You Need All Senses" are published by HarperCollins. Boris Pfeiffer has been writing poetry since he was 13 years old. The books „Lockdown - a C-Movie" and „Gravitationen, vol 1: Nicht aus Adams Rippe" with pictures by the painter Michèle Meister are published by Akademie-der-Abenteuer, Berlin.

Kheder Salfij, A Syrian Kurdish poet, born in 1963, holds a PhD in Arts, works as a professor of modern Arabic literature at Sofia University - Bulgaria, and worked as an editor in the Arabic section of the Bulgarian National Radio. He is the author of three collections of poetry (The Tired Rose Dinner, Blue Foxes, The Body in the Blue of His Absence, if you kill the way you kill my heart) in addition to many of his academic studies (The Religious and the Secular in Modern Arabic Poetry).

Agron Shele, was born in October 7th, 1972, in the Village of Leskaj, city of Permet, Albania. Is the author of the following literary works: "The Steps of Clara" (Novel), "Beyond a grey curtain" (Novel), "Wrong Image" (novel), "Innocent Passage" (poetry), White stones (poetry) RIME SPARSE-Il suono di due voci poetiche del Mediterraneo (Poesie di Agron Shele e Claudia Piccinno), La mia Musa ("Libri di-versi in diversi libri" – Italy, 2020); Murmure d'un autre monde (poetry), Klisania, Queen of the lake (Short story) and "Ese-I and Ese-II)". Agron Shele is also the coordinator of International Anthologies: "Open Lane-1", "Pegasiada, Open Lane-2, ATUNIS magazine (Nr 1, 2, 3, 4, 5, 6, 7, 8)" and Atunis Galaxy Anthology 2018, 2019, 2020, 2021, 2022, 2023. He is the winner of some international literary prizes. Is a member of the Albanian Association of Writers, member of the World Writers Association, in Ohio, United States, Poetas del Mundo, WPS, Unione world Poetry and the President of the International Poetical Galaxy "Atunis". He is published in many newspapers, national and international magazines, as well as published in many global anthologies: Almanac 2008, 2017; World Poetry Yearbook 2009, 2013, 2015, The Second Genesis-2013, Kibatek 2015-Italy, Metafora (Poland), Keleno-Greece, etc. Currently resides in Belgium and continues to dedicate his time and efforts in publishing literary works with universal values.

Andy Siege, Andy Siege, born as Andreas Madjid Siege in Kenya in 1985, is a German/Iranian film director and writer. His debut feature film "Beti and Amare" which he wrote and directed was nominated for multiple high profile international film awards. He is also the author of various books. He has a BA in Creative Writing and an MA in Political Science. Currently, Andy lives in Frankfurt, Germany.

Nasrin Siege, *1950 in Tehran, author of books for children and young people, poet, collector of fairy tales, psychologist, came to Germany with her parents and siblings at the age of eight, grew up in Hamburg and Flensburg, studied in Kiel, worked as a psychotherapist in Friedrichsdorf/ Taunus. From 1983 to 2016, she lived in Africa. Since October 2016 Nasrin Siege has been living in Germany. In 1996, she founded the association „Hilfe für Afrika e.V." (Help for Africa) with which she still supports projects in various African countries. Many of her books are about children and childhood in Africa. Her first poems date back to the early 60s. With them she soon discovered the healing effect of poetry in dealing with one's own identity after separation, loss, and living between and in different worlds. Some of her poems have appeared in anthologies. In 2022, her first volume of poetry, Almonds and Raisins," was published by a German publisher. Awards, 2022 Federal Cross of Merit 1st Class of the Federal Republic of Germany. 2006 Two Wings Award (Austria).1993 Children's Book Award of the Commissioner for Foreigners of the Berlin Senate.More about Nasrin Siege can be found here: www.nasrin-siege.com. More about Hilfe für Afrika e.V. can be found here: www.hilfefuerafrika.de

Antje Stehn, Germany, resides in Italy. Poet, visual artist, art curator, member of German Exil-PEN. Since 1980 she has been showing her art work in international exhibitions around Europe and the US. Since 2014 she is organizing poetic-artistic performances. She is part of the international Collective „Poetry is my Passion". Co-editor of the poetry magazine TamTamBumBum, Los Ablucionistas and Teerandaz. She is member of the direction committee of the Piccolo Museo della Poesia of Piacenza, Italy. In 2022 she published her most recent bilingual book "Grotesk" with Expeditionen Verlag. Her poems are translated into eleven different languages and published in numerous international Antologies. Since 2020 she is curating the art-poetry project "Rucksack a Global Poetry Patchwork which involves more than 250 international poets.

Annabel Villar (Montevideo, Uruguay/ Spain), Poet and cultural activist. Founding member Liceo Poetico de Benidorm; Associate Academic and Honorary Member American Academy of Modern Literature; Director "Azul" Poetry Collection and International Poetry Festival „Benidorm & Costa Blanca"; Founding Member Student Academy of Contemporary Art (Rio de Janeiro, Brazil, Chair No. 6 „Gabriela Mistral") Author of "Viaje al Sur del Sur" (2015), "Cantar la Vida" (XVI Provincial Poetry Prize of Aspe, Alicante, 2015), "Meditación" (bilingual Spanish-English, 2017) and "Claustrofobia & Vértigo "((bilingual Spanish-English, 2018)

Peter Voelker, (73) was born in Gruendau- Rothenbergen (Germany). After qualifying as a Certified Forwarding Agent, he worked in all branches of the Transport Industry. He wrote and edited there for 2 years as the Responsible Editor in the Foreign Trade Department. During this time, he was in contact with the Hamburg workshop of the „Werkkreis Literature Arbeitswelt "(Literature Workshop working world). From 1982 to 1989 he was the Responsible Editor for European Politics in the news agency United Economic Service (vwd) in Eschborn/Germany. Towards the end of the eighties, he became co-editor of the alternative magazine „Neue Hanauer Zeitung "(nhz). Together with political friends he established the „Solidaritaetsfonds demokratischer Medien in der Welt e.V., Goeppingen "in 1993. This organization supports independent media and art projects throughout the world. At present he is a member of the directorate. From November 1989 to March 2007, he was the General Secretary of the Media and Film Department of the German Media Trade Union in Stuttgart and Berlin. In this capacity he wrote several articles for books on the future of the media. He was one of the artists of the „Kulturstation Kaufmann"in Gelnhausen / Germany. During the past 15 years he publicized 18 books of lyric poetry. In the year 2014 he got the great award of poetry for his book "Agamemnon and Kassandra in Lakonia" from the International Academy of Arts "Orient – Occident" (Rumania).

Nahid Ensafpour, (Iran, Germany, 1961), She is a bilingual writer, poet and translator, who was born in Tehran. Since 1985 she lives in Germany/Köln. In April 2015, she completed the correspondence course „Literary Writing" at the Cornelia Goethe Academy, Frankfurt/Main and graduated with a diploma. She studied New German Literature and Philosophy at the Fern-Universität Hagen. Her poems have been published in numerous German and international anthologies. Many of her poems have been translated into several languages. She is a member of the World Writers' Association „Licio Poetico de Benidorm", as well as a member of the Schiller Association Leipzig and the Hainburger Writers' Association Austria. She is a member of PEN Club in Austria. In 2016, she was a prize winner at the poetry festival in Rödermark/Germany.

At the age of 18, she was privileged to enjoy Persian vocal training. In Germany she received vocal training in classical and solfège from 2008-2012.

She has published the following:

(2014) Book of poems „Brennende Sehnsucht",

(2016) Poetry collection „Gesang des Augenblicks",

(2018) Poetry collection published together with Peter Völker „Sonnentanz und Nachtschatten",

(2019) Book of poems „Leise weht das Wort dahin," Engelsdorfer Leipzig publishing,

(2020) Book of poems „Poetry overcomes boundaries",

(2021) „LebensLichtSpuren" a joint work with three authors from Austria (Erwin Matl), Germany (Peter Völker) und Brazil (Viviane de Santana).

Aus dem Verlag:

Mandeln und Rosinen
Gedichte und Bilder

Auf diesen Seiten
findest du
singende Fische
Perlengeschichten
verwoben-alt
trinkst goldenen Tee
lauschst dem Echo
der Sehnsucht
denn mittendrin
im Leben
süß und auch bitter
sind Mandeln und Rosinen.

Taschenbuch
136 Seiten
ISBN 978-3985301188

Nasrin Siege / Maryam Andaz

Nicht aus Adams Rippe

Gravitationen 1 von 4

Die in Australien lebende Künstlerin Michèle Meister und der in Deutschland lebende Kinderbuchautor und Dichter Boris Pfeiffer legen nach ihrem Punk Band „Lockdown - ein C-movie" den ersten von vier Bänden ihres Werks aus Malerei und Gedicht der Jahre 1979 bis heute vor: „Nicht aus Adams Rippe".

In den Gedichten des ersten Bandes: Das Aufwachsen eines Jungen in Berlin, das Mannwerden, das Menschwerden, Liebe, Einsamkeit, Sehnsucht nach der verlorenen, weitentfernten Mutter, Begegnungen in der Großstadt, Streifzüge in die Generationen, Menschengestalten, Naturfetzen und urbane Details mit Liebe und Offenheit. In den Bildern in tiefer weiblicher Perspektive Traumschwere Visionen voller Zärtlichkeit und Härte, öffnende Hingebungen ans Leben, farbbeseelte Aufschreie, Geschenke der Empfängnis, Bildergeburten der eigenen Identität und der der anderen, bereit für das Entsetzen wie für die Liebe, bereit, uns mitfühlen zu lassen, uns frei zu lassen.

Broschiert
158 Seiten
ISBN 978-3985301218

Michèle Meister / Boris Pfeiffer